METAMORPHOSIS
A Motivational Memoir of Self-Healing, Transformation, and Successful Manifestation

ASHLEY NOEL

Black Rose Writing | Texas

©2023 by Ashley Noel
All rights reserved. No part of this book may be reproduced, stored in a retrieval system or transmitted in any form or by any means without the prior written permission of the publishers, except by a reviewer who may quote brief passages in a review to be printed in a newspaper, magazine or journal.

The author grants the final approval for this literary material.

First printing

The author has tried to recreate events, locales and conversations from his/her memories. In order to maintain anonymity in some instances, the author may have changed the names of individuals and places. The author may have changed some identifying characteristics and details such as physical properties, occupations and places of residence.

ISBN: 978-1-68513-096-1
PUBLISHED BY BLACK ROSE WRITING
www.blackrosewriting.com

Printed in the United States of America
Suggested Retail Price (SRP) $20.95

Metamorphosis is printed in Sabon

*As a planet-friendly publisher, Black Rose Writing does its best to eliminate unnecessary waste to reduce paper usage and energy costs, while never compromising the reading experience. As a result, the final word count vs. page count may not meet common expectations.

Editor: Jennifer Caven, Mainly Words

Dedicated to my children, De'Andre and Amaya. Always follow your dreams and never give up. And to you, the reader. May *Metamorphosis* bring you inspiration, desire, healing, peace, and more.

Praise for **METAMORPHOSIS**

"Ashley's story gives hope and inspiration to all of us. She reminds me of how I finally took control of my life and used the same basic principles she used to overcome addiction, depression, and bad mental habits that keep people from realizing their true potential."
–Dave Dahl, Creator & Co-Founder, Dave's Killer Bread
(Former Addict, Ex-Con, Current Musician and Entrepreneur)

"Ashley Noel's story is one of resilience, strength, grace, fortitude, and proof beyond any doubt that one can change their life no matter how deep the grief or how steep the climb. This isn't just a memoir but a guide to change, a guide to true *Metamorphosis*."
–Kim Conrey, author of *Stealing Ares, Book One in the Ares Ascending series.*

"The section in *Metamorphosis* about encountering angel numbers for the first time is exciting to read! Experiencing angel numbers is the strongest indicator of being connected to spirit and or spirit guides. Noel's account of how she discovered the numbers, learned their meaning, and used them as a guidance tool, is inspiring for others who are looking to do the same."
–Gina Self, Certified Psychic Medium

"Ashley's writing style allows you to truly feel every single aspect of emotion from her incredible "Metamorphosis." Triumph and euphoria, pain, and frustration. Then… the unspeakable tragedy of the loss of her son's father and her spiral into despair. I felt it, you'll feel it too. Ashley's story is one of constant comebacks that culminates in victory over heartache. Victory that you will feel in your bones from her deep, soulful writing style. You will experience every emotion reading her book. If you don't… check your pulse."
–Mike Violette, Maine Radio Personality

"A vivid and vulnerable account of a triumphant tale that takes you through a range of emotions. I was invested from the first word until the last."
–Dr. La Toya Davis

"In her spiritual memoir, Ashley bravely shares the truth of her struggles, addiction and a tragic loss. She doesn't stop there, either in her life or her sharing.... she offers hope and inspiration to others struggling to create the life they desire and are meant to live by showing how she paid attention to the support, guidance and healing offered her at one of the most difficult times of her life. Keep an eye out for further sharings from Noel; she has a message to share and won't stop until she reaches as many people as she can."
–Martha Williams, shamanic practitioner

"The world needs nothing more than a true, vulnerable story share that exemplifies the rawness of what it means to be human. Bound to touch lives."
–Amanda Monty | Co-CEO, Topset Meals. Yoga teacher. Trauma survivor.

"Ashley Noel has written a great book on self-help that I thoroughly enjoyed. The author goes into details about her journey in her memoir. Like most of us in our lives, Ashley had her ups and downs, but in the final analysis she used spiritual forces in nature to become the person she wished to create. Use this book and Noel's experience to change your life for the creation of a new person that you will be proud to become."
–Don Green, CEO of The Napoleon Hill Foundation.

Acknowledgments

First and foremost, I want to thank my mom, Velvet Noel, and my dad, Mark McIlwain, for creating me and supporting me always. Mom, you have been my biggest fan ever since I was little, and I am blessed to call you Mom!

To my children, De'Andre and Amaya, thank you for motivating me to always be my best and to never give up. Everything I do is all for you!

A *big* thank you to my publisher, Black Rose Writing, for believing in my work and providing me with the opportunity to share *Metamorphosis* with the world.

To those who guided me throughout my writing process—Jennifer Caven, Jennifer Allen, Juliette Guilmette, my mother, Velvet, and stepmother, Cheryl McIlwain—I couldn't have done it without you! I appreciate all your support, suggestions, and editing skills. Every one of you pushed me to be my best, and I am a better writer today because of it.

To my author mentors whom I mention in the book, thank you for inspiring me to write again.

And to my dear friend, Anna Foster. You who started it all, encouraging me to read a book that ended up changing my life indefinitely, and I am forever grateful.

I'd also like to thank my team of spirit guides and guardian angels for their constant support.

Finally, I'd like to acknowledge my Gram, aunt, and closest family members and friends who have watched me grow and heal over the last ten years. Each one of you has helped me in some way during my darkest moments, and I love you all so much for it. Thank you.

METAMORPHOSIS

Introduction

You are amazing. You are strong; you are special, and I congratulate you for taking the first step in changing your life. Sometimes we feel stranded, stuck in the past, or an unsatisfying present. Sometimes we feel lost, searching for a direction to take. *Metamorphosis* is a guidance tool created through my personal experience with soul-searching, to help bring you back to your path of purpose and to living your best life.

The book you are about to read contains my true story of ups, downs, everything in between, and how I rediscovered myself. *Metamorphosis* is written in three sections. Section One briefly talks about my time of addiction prior to motherhood and the accident that upended my life. I then offer raw insights into the collapse of my mental health and how being stuck in an impossibly deep hole can subsequently create a ladder for you to climb back into the light. The material in Section One may generate a deep, emotional reflection of your own wounds, but this is good. Developing awareness of our hidden wounds can give birth to new desires within us.

In Section Two, I reflect on my current situation, my childhood, and how a dear friend offered a new perspective of life and the Universe in the pages of one simple book. I talk about my discovery of the Law of Attraction, self-healing, and principles for success that helped bring my wildest dreams to fruition. It is important to read Section Two with a clear, open mind to absorb everything that is presented. This section talks about commitment to transformation.

Finally, Section Three will share the spiritual phenomena I experienced when, having let go of my past through reflection and self-healing, I allowed the mystical world of guardian angels and spirit guides into my life as helpers.

I learned from well-known spiritual pioneers and employed the natural forces of the Universe. However, I warn you, once you understand and accept all that is being presented in *Metamorphosis*, there is no turning back. Everything you once knew—the world, your life, the people around you—will appear different. The new awareness of universal magic and spiritual help will positively change your life in ways you couldn't imagine . . . until now. Remember, you are not alone in this life-changing journey, so relax, learn, and trust in the purpose that is within us all and the ability to self-create.

Well wishes,
Ashley

Section One

Reflection

At seventeen, I experienced my first epiphany, which irrevocably altered the path I had intended to take. As I cruised over an old bridge, riding passenger in my high school boyfriend's car, a clear and unfamiliar voice spoke to me.

I repeated the message quietly under my breath: "You're not meant to go to Johnson and Wales; you're supposed to be a writer." At first, the message relayed confused me, but after the confusion passed, an overwhelming sensation came over me. I didn't question it, and I didn't fear it. A higher power was opening my mind to what I needed to hear. I didn't know what I was supposed to write about, but I trusted and believed in the message I'd received. Too nervous to share what I experienced with my boyfriend, I kept quiet but vowed to fulfill my purpose one day and become a writer.

When the last month of high school arrived, I dropped out of Johnson and Wales to follow my fate. The only downfall to bypassing college was that I was too naïve to realize what would happen if I didn't immediately follow through with my promise. While my friends were enjoying their freshman year of college, I moved an hour away from home, found a job, and got high on whatever I could get my hands on.

While I was growing up, my mother kept a firm hand on my activities. I felt smothered at times, like most teens, so I took advantage of being on my own and explored my freedom in ways I never expected. I took a job waiting tables at a local strip club and kept it hidden from my divorced, conservative parents. I made friends with the dancers, discovering new drug connections along the way.

I spent my rent money on popping pills, cocaine, Amato's sandwiches (when I ate), and Camel Turkish Golds, since I had picked up the bad habit of chain-smoking. After ten months, broke and weighing a hundred pounds, I was back at home, stuck in a shit town, with nothing to show for my freedom.

Unfortunately, it wasn't enough to make me realize I had screwed up, and I kept the drug party going for the next couple of years. At age twenty, I decided it was time for a fresh start and gave writing another shot. I changed my location drastically and moved over fifteen hundred miles away to Michigan to be closer to my then-boyfriend, thinking that his journey was mine and that I could write anywhere.

To my dismay, the big move brought me zero success. Instead of plugging away at the keyboard, I spent my time snorting narcotics with my drug-dealing neighbors. I ruined my one and only "on the spot" job interview at Hooters because I was too high to process a basic question. The manager asked if I had a superpower, what would it be? I replied without hesitation, "To have lots of shoes."

When the fifteen-hundred-dollar bank loan my mother cosigned ran out six weeks after arriving, I returned home once again. After my second failed attempt at becoming a writer, I still wasn't motivated enough to create a change for the better.

I continued to live my life like a drug-induced version of *Groundhog Day*, reliving the same mistakes over and over again, until at twenty-one, I hit bottom for the first time.

Knee-deep in drug and alcohol addiction, I blew through a small inheritance my grandfather left me: twelve thousand dollars bought me a used car, a shitload of coke, several bundles of heroin, and a sack of OxyContins. The icing on top of the drug cake I had baked from scratch? Many liters of Jägermeister to wash it all down.

I spent every night partying, sometimes staying up for days. The coke kept me awake, and the pills made me tolerable to be around when I was coming down. The liquor was the perfect size cherry to compliment my daily self-prescribed sundae. Every day I got high in the bathroom at work, attempting to numb the pain of failure. It was the only thing that helped me accept the direction I had chosen instead of fulfilling my destiny.

With two failed moves under my belt, zero books written, and not a single cent in my bank account, I was waiting tables part time and living in my mother's basement with no plans or goals. It was eating me alive. I was angry about spending my grandfather's money so carelessly, and I knew he would have been disappointed. So I handled my poor decision-making the only way I knew how . . . with more poor decision-making.

I traded belongings and fronted drugs I didn't have money for. Recognizing that I had nothing to pay back at the end of the week for what I had borrowed, I hoped the dealers would forget about my debts.

The only other thing that brought me peace was cruising around town in my Nissan Altima, cigarette in hand and sunroof open to the world. I felt untouchable. Every terrible choice I had made escaped through the 15x30 inch window facing the sky as I sped down Main Street.

The rumbling bass of music bouncing about in my chest, mixed with teasing thoughts I had become hot stuff, allowed me the freedom of being what I had dreamt about, even if it wasn't true. I felt like a rock star tucked away in the comfort of my compact car, flipping off the small town holding me captive as I let the crevices of my fingers chase the wind through the open window.

It wasn't until six months later, when an unexpected seed grew into a blossoming human life, that I finally changed. I chose the life of my unborn child over the drugs I loved so much. That was the first time my son saved me.

With a wonderful support system to help me stay on track with sobriety, I gave the idea of family a chance. My new boyfriend, Damin, whom I met in high school, was drug free and completely against being with anyone using anything stronger than the natural green herb (marijuana). With his help, I succeeded and embraced the new chance in life I was given with thanks.

Overcoming that addictive period cold turkey had me feeling strong and untouchable. As a mother, I felt complete, as if life had purpose again. I came face to face with my life-changing moment and figured it would be smooth sailing from there on out.

I started college in the fall after my son's first birthday and four years later, with one semester left before graduation, I was ready to face the world and the book of short stories my professor and mentor had been encouraging me to write. With six years of sobriety to show for, the world was my oyster. Little did I know the Universe had set a terrible trial for me.

ASHLEY NOEL

Death Becomes Her

To this day, I'll never know for sure if he was sleeping at the time of impact. It makes it easier to think that he was. Whenever I wondered if he watched the safe space shrink between him and the oncoming truck until that last second, it was unbearable. Visualizing him with his eyes closed always carried a sense of comfort.

The first in his family to graduate from college, Damin prided himself on his work ethic. He put in a minimum of sixty hours a week and wore the title of lineman proudly. Whether working in the scorching summer sun or the frigid Maine winters, his days were always long and tiring.

To help lighten the load of the sixteen-hour days ahead of them, the guys on his crew often carpooled. They left so early in the morning that whoever was riding passenger would try to get some shuteye. I was hesitant to have him riding with other people. One day, I asked if that was the best route for him. He assured me it was, and that everybody did it. He told me no matter who he was riding with, he would be safe.

Three months later, in the early morning hours after the sun had risen, I had just started my first load of laundry and was preparing to bring our son to preschool when I got the call. There had been an accident. I froze in the middle of my kitchen, not knowing what to do. I'll never forget the sound of the work supervisor's voice, low-toned and filled with sympathy. He explained he knew of no one's condition and that an ambulance had taken them to the nearest hospital.

I hung up the phone and began pacing back and forth, trying to gather my thoughts without alerting my son. I felt sick to my stomach. All I could hear was a loud ringing in my ears. Inside, I knew it was bad. It didn't matter that they wouldn't give me any information over the phone. I knew what had happened would change my life.

I looked out the living room window and watched the snowflakes fall gently from the sky. The expected storm was not far behind. After the initial shock wore off, my adrenaline kicked into high gear. I brought De'Andre upstairs to his bedroom and turned his TV on, setting the volume on high.

I raced back downstairs to Damin's family and then called my mother at work. The plan was to drop De'Andre off at preschool, and then the three of us—Damin's mother, my mother, and I—would drive to the emergency room and meet the rest of the family there. I sat down and calmed my breath the best I could while waiting for the others to come, but it helped a little. Watching the seconds tick by on the clock, I grew queasier with every passing moment. The snow was falling faster, and the realization that we would have to drive slowly erupted a raging frustration inside me.

When we eventually got on the road and started driving south to the hospital, I received a second phone call and was told to keep driving. He was headed farther south by ambulance, unable to be life-flighted due to weather, to a trauma center in Portland, and they urged us to get there fast.

Normally, it only took a little over an hour to make the drive to Portland, but the farther we drove, the thicker the snow became, making it hard to drive safely. It was a good thing that my friend and neighbor let us borrow her vehicle with studded tires. There's no telling how much longer it would have taken without it.

During the trip south, waiting to be with him, all I could do was pray. I clutched the black, beaded rosary my mother had given me between my sweaty fingers and asked God for a miracle. I kept repeating that everything would be fine, but I knew better. Telling lies to myself was the only form of self-comfort I could manage.

From the passenger window, I watched the snowflakes continue to fall and wondered if it was snowing in Heaven. In the back seat, his mother sobbed for the son she had seen just the day before. I reached back and offered my hand for her to hold. She clenched it tightly and began stroking the top of my cold, clammy hand, and together we prayed.

When we finally arrived at the hospital, a counselor, a surgeon, and a nurse greeted us. I fainted in the tiny room they offered us after I was told that he had not regained consciousness. At that point, it had been hours since the collision.

The impact from the Jeep Cherokee they were riding in, which had hit the fully loaded logging truck head on, had caused his head injury. The surgeon put his hand on my back. He informed me they had a few more tests to run, but that it didn't look good.

As I sat there, digesting what I had just been told, I had a strange, out-of-body experience. I could feel my body sitting in the wheelchair that they had quickly rushed me into when I fainted, but I wasn't there. I was looking down at my limp limbs in the chair as it sat in the center of the tiny room.

I could hear the doctors tell our mothers that the driver wasn't wearing a seatbelt and that he had gone through the window and miraculously survived. His body frozen and paralyzed, but his mind was awake. It was ironic that the one wearing the seatbelt was unconscious and the one who wasn't was wide awake.

We could see him while the doctors ran their tests. The time passed slowly, and the larger empty waiting room they transferred us to was filling with family and friends. One by one we filed into his hospital room, taking turns with the inevitable goodbye that we were waiting for doctors to confirm.

I held his still, scuffed hand between both of mine. I leaned in to smell it before kissing it. It didn't smell alive anymore. It smelled of bandages and medical tubing that bulged from his lifeless grip.

Just hours before, I had seen that very hand grip the banister in our bedroom before running downstairs to leave for work.

That morning, I had been too tired to say goodbye, too tired to suggest he drive himself to work instead of carpooling, because the weather was going to be bad. Listening to the sounds of the machine pumping air into his lungs, I couldn't help but wonder if I could have prevented this. If I wasn't too fucking lazy to lift my head up off my pillow to speak, would he not be lying there? Could I have slowed down time just enough to place him in a unique position on the road, one where the truck was ahead of them and not passing them?

I sat in the room, staring at the bandage wrapped around his head. I was devastated, and I felt even worse when I began scanning every horrible memory we had shared. I remembered every time we went to bed angry, every time I told him I hated him, and every time we argued about some insignificant issue. And in that very moment, I hated myself because he was lying there.

I hated that our family was in a position that couldn't be fixed. I hated I was waiting to hear if he would ever open his beautiful eyes again. I hated wondering if I'd be able to apologize for all the rotten things I had ever said to him. No matter how much fussing and fighting we had experienced in our six years together, we loved each other more than the angry words we sometimes shared. We were young when we became parents, just kids ourselves. We did the best we could and stuck together through everything.

Just as I was cursing my negative memories, the doctors came in and said they needed to speak to everyone. The moment we had been waiting for arrived. I walked out of his room and couldn't help but notice the many pairs of eyes staring at me from behind the nurse's station. I could sense their reluctance to make actual eye contact with me as I walked by them and headed toward the waiting room. They quickly looked down and away before flashing their kindest smiles at me. Their smiles were clear indicators of what we were about to hear, and my heavy heart plummeted even further in my chest.

Our families and friends gathered round, filling the chairs in the waiting room. We sat with straight posture and silenced voices and waited patiently for the doctor to speak up. A young man dressed in wrinkled, navy blue scrubs excused himself through the crowd and made his way to where I was sitting. He pushed his medium length hair behind his ears and gently sighed before telling me how sorry he was, but that Damin was brain dead and would never wake or be the same again. All his other organs were working, but the trauma from the impact was too much for him to heal from.

I regarded the doctor with confusion. I didn't understand what he had said. I felt as if I were back in Catholic elementary school, staring at my kindergarten teacher, asking her to explain the concepts of simple arithmetic. It didn't add up. Everything else worked but his brain?

I felt the anger rising inside of me. I was furious at his fate, and as our combined families stood together in unity, they watched as I erupted. I stood up and began kicking and screaming like an angry toddler in reaction to what the doctors said. With my hands flailing about, I reached for the closest thing to me, the chair. I bent down, picked it up, and hurled it across the room.

My father raced over to me and held me down while everyone watched as I lay on the floor screaming for mercy. I remember looking at my mother for comfort, as she's always known what to say to me when I've been afraid. I laid my sobbing head in her lap and begged her to tell me why this was happening. She wept with me as she stroked my head, feeling helpless and not knowing what to say.

I listened to the sound of everybody's tears falling heavily from their eyes and looked over to the priest who had sat with us hoping to comfort our aching hearts. With my eyes fixated on the white collar around his neck, I screamed at him, telling him how angry

I was with God. I yelled at him how I didn't understand why God wanted this to happen. Why would he take him from us? Why would he leave my son without his father?

With pity in his glance, he placed his palm on my shaking shoulder and told me that God's ways were greater than what we'd ever know. He told me it was okay to be angry and that it wasn't our job to figure out the tragedies in life, but to trust God and know that he will see us through. I stared back at him with a blank face and frozen eyes, unable to accept his pronouncement. I wept as he placed his other hand on my back and listened to his deep voice as he prayed.

After taking two Xanax from my friend, I settled down enough to make my way back to Damin's room and sit with him one last time. Still, I couldn't grasp why the doctors couldn't save him. I cried over him and told him how much I loved him. I thanked him for giving me our son and told him how proud I was of him. Then I leaned in, kissed him, and said goodbye.

The drive home was quiet. My phone full of texts, missed calls, and voicemails, all sought answers. I couldn't return a single one of them. All I could think about was my son and that his father was never coming home.

A family friend had picked De'Andre up at school and spent the night at their house. I didn't know what to expect when I got to the hospital, and traveling with a five-year-old in a snowstorm didn't seem safe or sensible.

I felt devastated as we traveled home on I-95, knowing what I would need to do shortly after sunrise. How would I tell him? How would I comfort him? Would he be angry that I hadn't allowed him to travel with us to say goodbye? The questions raced around the endless track in my head the entire drive home. I couldn't focus on anything. I wanted to sleep and not wake up.

That night, I shared a bed with my mother at her house. I slept little, and at one point she woke me to ask if I was okay. I had been calling out for Damin in my sleep. Every time I woke, I felt disoriented about where I was, and then when I remembered, I tightly closed my eyes again, hoping to wake up in my bed with him annoyingly snoring next to me.

The next morning came fast. My mother was up before me, and when she heard me stirring, she calmly walked in and twisted the blinds open. The bright sun glisten off the freshly fallen snow. I couldn't cry and I couldn't think. All I could do was lie there, trying to figure out how the day was bright with light when all I felt was darkness.

Just then, I heard a gentle tapping on the screen door. It was De'Andre. Listening to his laughter greet my mother at the door, I began silently sobbing into the pillow. I was about to break the heart of the person I loved most, and I was petrified.

Summoning a small bit of courage, I sat up and patted my eyes dry with the comforter. I swallowed the lump in my throat as I listened to his little footsteps running excitedly toward the bedroom. Like a fireball shooting out of a cannon, he burst through the door and jumped onto the bed. He fell into my arms and smothered me with hugs. I held him for a minute, enjoying the happiness that flowed from him. He kissed me on the cheek and flopped down beside me. I kissed him back on his forehead and told him I had something to tell him.

As his deep brown eyes gazed up at me, I felt as though he already knew something was wrong. He immediately asked me where his daddy was, and with the strength of God, I dug down deep and worked up enough courage to find the words.

I explained how the previous day before the storm, his daddy was driving to work and there had been an accident. I told him that his daddy got hurt and that the doctors tried to help him but couldn't. I went on to explain that he was in Heaven with the angels and that he wasn't coming home.

He broke down, crying hysterically. As he wailed and whimpered, he bravely asked, "So we'll never be a family again?" It broke my heart to hear him say that. In that moment, I felt completely helpless as a mother watching my child cry, knowing there was little I could do to comfort him.

In my mother's bedroom, I sat in the same position as she had held me the day before, crying and holding my child. With his small body shaking beneath mine, I squeezed him tighter until he stopped. He cried for about twenty minutes before walking out of the room on his own and asking for a juice box. My mother passed him his favorite beverage, Apple Juicy Juice. His fingers clenched the small carton as he made his way to a picture of his father that sat on a decorated shelf my mother had filled with family pictures. With the memory of his father in hand, he went into the living room, switched on the TV, and sat down on the couch.

Afraid to return home alone, I spent just shy of two weeks at my mother's house. I knew eventually I'd have to leave, but I was so fearful of being alone. The day I finally went home, leaving De'Andre with my mother so I could explore on my own, it felt different. It felt dark, and the radiant energy that used to radiate through the three-story townhouse had turned ominous. Signs of his life were left everywhere: his shoes at the door; his work sunglasses on the kitchen table, waiting to be picked up on the next sunny day; his favorite hat left hanging on the wall hook.

I cried with every step I took as I forced my way through the townhouse. I could smell him everywhere, and in my head, I could hear his loud feet on the hardwood floor after tracking in mud all over my black carpet like he always did after work. Sobbing loud enough for my neighbors to hear through the thin walls, I slowly made my way upstairs to our bedroom.

I climbed to the top of the steps on my knees, placed my hand on the banister where I saw him last, and wept uncontrollably. I couldn't contain the surge of emotion washing over me. It was more than I could bear! I dropped to the floor and began crawling over to his closet. I peeled back the slightly open door and flung myself inside. His smell lingered heavy, making me miss him that much more. I grabbed and pulled at the sleeves of his sweatshirts, trying to sit up as tall as I could. The stinging from my rug-burned knees demanded my attention.

Too weak to stand, too feeble to pull myself up, I collapsed, ripping down his clothes along with me. Pleading for his return, I threw my body into the heap of tangled clothes and gripped them as tightly as I could. I screamed into the fabric that had once clothed his living body and yelled out for him to hold me. I pleaded for him to come back to us.

As I lay on the carpet, I looked up at the popcorn ceiling, tears running down my face. I had never experienced so much pain in my life as I did in that moment of accepting he was really gone and never coming home. Even though I'd seen him for the last time at the hospital, my brain could not process his death that day. Lost in emotion on my bedroom floor, I accepted he was gone and that my son and I now lived alone. It was the first step in understanding that what had happened was real, and I hated it.

With my arms and legs spread out wide like a starfish, I dug deep for the smallest bit of strength I could find and rolled over. I pulled my limp frame up the best I could, gripped the bumpy carpet beneath me, and clawed my way toward the bed. I looked around at our bedroom as I felt my legs dragging slowly behind me. As I inched my way closer and closer to my destination, I knew it would be a long time before anything ever seemed okay again.

Not wanting to give up, I reached for the L.L. Bean down comforter draped over the edge of our bed. I clutched the heavy cluster of encased feathers and lifted my grieving body up. To my surprise, I succeeded. As soon as I conquered the mountain of fabric, I plopped down, took a deep breath, and shut my eyes. Maybe I was stronger than I thought.

Fight or Flight

I realize now more than ever just how traumatic a single incident can be in a person's life. What's far more telling is how a human reacts to the trauma. My reaction evoked the "fight or flight" mechanism in me. Even now, as I attempt to weed out the last vestiges of poison still living inside me, I'm tempted to run and hide in the closet like I used to.

After the accident, De'Andre's walk-in closet was the only place I could seek solitude to cry in private. I never wanted my son to see the tears that sporadically spilled from my eyes whenever I sensed the agony pouring in. Brave and stubborn most of my life, I had never run from anything until Damin died. I see how it was easier to take flight, as I wanted nothing to do with what had happened. It was easier to pretend it was just a hellish nightmare than to accept what was and learn how to cope with it.

No one can ever prepare you for handling grief. How I dealt with it was the turning point for me and the direction I fled in after the wake and funeral. How I handled the grief and the pressure I put on myself to do so was the beginning of a dark tale, soon to be filled with many monsters.

Only specific segments of the first few weeks remained in my subconscious. When I tried to assemble the pile of the snapshots together into a memory, it seemed like flashes of images frozen in time. The one occasion that held strong was the smell of vomit on the neckline of my dress shirt after I had struggled to wipe it clean at the funeral home. And when it was time to let in the guests from outside, I sat slumped in an antique chair with wooden arms scrolled like a throne while family members and friends walked by to pay their respects. I distracted myself the best I could and dug my nails deep into the grooves of the chair. I sobbed and asked my mother to pass me more of my anxiety pills as people flooded through the doors.

She shook out the recommended dose into my sweaty palms. I didn't care who saw the pills being dumped into my greedy hands. All I wanted was something to dull my senses. Even though everything else seemed like a bad dream, the internal pain was the only thing that reminded me I was still alive. Convinced I would never be the same, I chewed the Lorazepam and swallowed the bitter pill with what little saliva I had.

With each person who passed, my tears grew heavier as they offered their condolences. At one point, I ran to the bathroom to vomit. The guilt, the shock, and the sadness were too much. As I wiped off the vomit splattered over the collar of my shirt, I wondered how I was ever going to get to a place in time that offered happiness. In my soul, it felt as if I grew colder and darker with each minute that passed, like the Devil's child born in the dead of night.

I observed the remnants of crackers and ginger ale swimming around in the toilet bowl before I flushed it, and then returned to the crowd. As I pushed through the army of sturdy linemen there to support the family of their union brother, everything was moving in slow motion, just like in the movies. I felt drugged from the pills, and with what limited sleep I'd had, I was dazed and far removed from the reality I once knew.

After a couple hours of sharing grief, I couldn't take it anymore. The reason I was there overwhelmed me and I was disoriented from my overuse of psychotropics. I asked for someone to take me home. Weak from heartache, I could no longer communicate. I refused to grapple with what was going on around me. So I left my son with our family and escaped to my mother's house and the solitude I craved.

My cousin dropped me off, and as I watched her bright headlights disappear down the driveway, I felt shame. There I sat on my mother's couch, alone, but in the company of my misery. I thought how, as a mother, I could have left my child behind at his father's wake. He wasn't alone but with members of both our families, but I still didn't understand why I had put my own needs before him.

Disgusted with myself, I ran to the toilet again and vomited at the fact I had left him behind. I realized I should have stayed and been the last person to leave. I told myself I was a horrible person and convinced my heart that I had failed him again. As I crouched over the ceramic bowl, I begged Damin and God to forgive the selfish act of placing my son second. It was frustrating to think of how weak I was. So I swallowed the feelings of guilt and shoved them down into the growing pile. I accepted the cowardly robe draped over my shameful shoulders and stripped away the remaining regret.

It was cold standing naked by the porcelain tub. I turned on the hot water and watched as it drained from the rusted shower head. With the steam floating up, hitting my face like morning fog dripping off dewy grass, I stepped in and let the burning water wash over me. I longed for strength and screamed out, searching for the bravery I so needed. Inside, I felt dead. I could feel my insides turn black and harden with every bitter breath I took. I couldn't shake the question of why? Why us?

My hand gently traced the outline of the shower knob. Then my gentle touch morphed into something more sinister. I angrily shut the water off and forcefully yanked back the plastic shower curtain. With the fire of hell raging inside me, I yelled out at the top of my lungs until they emptied. I gasped for air to refill them, hoping to feel more alive. But I felt miserable, cold, and anything but human.

Desperate to turn back the hands of time to a happier place, I reached for the orange bottle of tiny white pills and devoured the courage I could not get any other way.

Wet with regret and guilt, I stood on the small bathmat and realized the medicine was quickly becoming my savior. My right-hand man. The pillow under my head. The Band-Aid over my cut. I wiped the condensation off the vanity mirror and looked at the ugliness that covered a once beautiful face. I stared at my reflection and wondered what I was about to become. I wondered if the old habits of drugs and alcohol I had given up years ago would come back to haunt me.

Dreading the days to follow, I told myself to hold it together long enough for the funeral. I needed to be strong for everyone to see, for my son to see. After that, I could sink into my pit of sorrow and drown in the sorrow that surrounded me.

The Funeral

The irony of waking up on the morning of the funeral to a beaming ball of sunshine, signifying the bright colors of life, was sickening. I watched the birds bathe themselves in the heat of the sun as it melted snow-covered roofs. Water trickling down the sides of houses made everything seem so normal. It was like nothing new was going on in the world, just another day. But to me, it wasn't. It was the day that marked the recognition of a death I wished to ignore.

When we pulled up to the packed church, with cars lining both sides of the street, I felt nauseous. I wanted to ask my cousin to turn around and floor it. I wanted to tell him I was too scared to go in and to take me home. I was too afraid to face people and too weak to watch the casket carrying my boyfriend roll past me. Feeling forced to attend a funeral I wasn't ready for, I got out of the car, swallowing the rising vomit desperate to escape, and forced my way to the front doors of the church.

I can't recall how I got to the wooden pew or who had brought me there to sit. I remember watching his friends and family carry the casket down the church aisle with De'Andre trailing behind. I remember watching them position it just right at the front of the church so everyone could see. I remember the white roses stretched across the top of the glossy, cherry wood casket. I remember the deafening crying that circulated through the church, and I remember the little hand that reached up to touch my shoulder to calm me as we listened to the sounds filling the house of God.

De'Andre's attempt to console me that day was the only motivation that got me to stagger up to the podium and speak.

Days before, I had sat at my mother's kitchen table and poured my heart out onto an intimidating blank piece of paper in front of me. With a number two pencil trembling between my fingers, I wrote words of honesty, love, and the valid intentions I had for raising our son the best way I knew how. I jammed the lead pencil as hard as I could into the white fibers of the paper. I felt angry as I tried my best to write a beautiful eulogy for the father of my son.

The more I wrote, the angrier I became. I knew that if I couldn't release some of the anger before I got up to speak, I would fail once again, running away like the coward I had been the night of the wake. So I reached for the only thing that hid the pain, another pill.

As I finished writing, I convinced myself that the only way I could ever read the letter was to take enough sedatives to put me in a hypnotic trance. Church was the last place I wanted to consume any form of drug, but felt I had no choice. I went into the kitchen and prepared a makeshift pill carrier that no one could detect, not even the priest.

Unwinding some Saran Wrap from the warped box, I took a few pills, placed them into the center of the wrap, and rolled it up into a tiny cocoon small enough to tuck into the tiny space where my bra met my breasts. I stared at the plastic package and was relieved to know that if I needed some pharmaceutical courage, I didn't need to pull out my bottle to do so. I could be discreet reaching in, clenching it tightly in my fist before unwrapping it gently. I didn't care what people thought. What I needed was seclusion when sharing a private moment of weakness was generally unobtainable at a funeral.

As I sat in the pew, awaiting my signal to speak, I remember having the same out-of-body experience I had felt that day in the waiting room. Nothing seemed real as I looked around the tightly packed church. It was hard to grasp the idea that soon I would go up and talk about the man I loved, the man I had known since age sixteen, and the man with whom I had spent the last six years of my life.

I had taken enough Lorazepam to knock out a normal person before I left the house, and the pills hidden in my bra stayed tightly secured in their makeshift plastic pill packet. I coached my chaotic mind to stay calm, knowing I was that much closer to delivering the eulogy. I paced my breath the best I could, attempting to slow my racing heart.

With a gentle nudge from my mother letting me know it was time, I pulled out my folded piece of paper and approached the podium. There, standing before a crowd whose faces expressed pity and sadness, I shared my written words. I spoke honestly about our relationship and that even though we weren't perfect, we still had loved one another. I spoke about his accomplishments and how I would raise our son to be honest and brave. I spoke about how strong I would be moving forward.

Deep down, I wanted to grab the microphone and bellow out how angry I was at him for dying. I wanted to scream to the crowd that I hated what our life was about to become. I wanted to shout and tell everyone that I was weak and hated being alone and how terribly I missed him. I wanted to cry out for someone to save me, but I couldn't. I looked at everybody and lied. Inside I was terrified of what was to come next. I could feel my sanity slipping away down a dark path, and that scared me more than anything.

After the funeral ended, we had an amazing gathering to celebrate his life and his accomplishments. Since we could not bury him in the heart of winter, everybody made their way to a restaurant for food and drinks. When we arrived, I snuck off to the bathroom, sat on the toilet, and cried. I felt drained and wanted solitude. I wiped the smeared mascara off my face and made my way to the bar, understanding I couldn't run away like I had days before.

I took one look at the bartender and asked for a double shot of Patrón Silver. I reached for the meds tucked away between my breasts and unwrapped them as he watched. I placed two pills in my mouth and grabbed the shot glass. He stood there staring at me, likely wondering what I was doing. I glared at him as I chucked back the shot, sucking down the dose along with it. With the empty glass tipped upside down, I slammed the brim of the tiny cup down onto the sticky table. I wiped the sour drippings from the corners of my mouth and walked away.

My mom told me it was important to greet those who came to the celebration, so I found a place near the door to stand, waiting to welcome guests as they arrived. The draft was cold as the door repeatedly opened. I stood slouched with my back against the wall. One after the other, people came in. It was impossible to keep up with the handshakes, so I nodded my head in recognition of those whose hands I couldn't shake.

I could feel the liquor and pills take effect with every motion I made. Like a hand pressed into soft clay, I sank against the wall that supported me, hoping it would hold me up long enough for me to acknowledge everyone.

As dark thoughts spun in my mind, I considered running out of the door and not looking back. I imagined leaving the gathering behind and fleeing to a place that offered seclusion, pills, and more Patrón.

It was easy to think of swallowing my emotions with old patterns of addiction, but the sound of De'Andre's footsteps running up behind me brought a bit of strength that enveloped me when I needed it most. He wrapped his little arms around my leg as his feet came to a halt. I rubbed his back and silently thanked the timing of his embrace. He had kept me from becoming a flight risk once again.

After twenty minutes at the door, I tried to return to where everyone was. My intoxication rising with each click of my high heels against the tile floor, I hoped I wouldn't slip and fall making a fool of myself. I could feel my stockings slide below my dress's hemline with each step I took. I paused for a moment and grasped the slippery fabric between my trembling fingers to pull them up.

I had no strength in my body. I was exhausted, drunk, and zoned out from the pills. My eyes welled up with tears of embarrassment. I felt sloppy as I stood in the middle of the open room. I wanted to pull myself together for my son, family, friends, and for Damin as well. I hated that both on the inside and out, I was a mess. All I wanted was a confident appearance to convince myself and others that, on a certain level, I had it together.

Just as I was about to burst out crying at the stubbornness of my black thigh-highs, I felt a gentle hand come from behind me and pull up my stocking. I turned around to see my good friend Samantha flash a kind smile at me as she reached over and pulled up the other one.

I'll never forget that moment. Out of all the memories I lost that day, her helping me was one that I'll always remember and appreciate. Her kindness meant more to me than she'll probably ever know. She made me feel that no matter how disheveled I was, someone would always be there for me. Even if it was just to pull up my stockings.

Self-Abuse

The first few weeks after the funeral were bad. When I'd wake up, the down comforter that once covered Damin and me gently while we slept had suddenly become a deep, contaminated sea of sharp sorrows. I fought desperately at every sunrise to raise my head above the murky depths.

Every morning when I pulled the comforter over me to cry, I could feel the disturbing thoughts of all that could go wrong in life wrapping around my ankles, weighing me down and pulling me under. After treading the dreadful waters, viciously trying to stay afloat, I would eventually make my way out of bed, wiping away the broken fragments of life from my eyes.

Things went south quickly after the accident. At first, when everything happened, I was so distraught that I couldn't eat, and when I tried, I would involuntarily vomit. After the funeral, once things settled, I still had the urge to throw up just about everything I swallowed. Only this time, it was voluntary. It was the only thing I could control.

Everything around me was spinning out of control and falling apart. Restricting what I ate somehow made me feel like I at least had one thing that no one could force or take away from me. I also was carrying an enormous amount of guilt for how I'd treated Damin before he died, and I didn't know how else to handle it.

Our relationship hadn't been picture-perfect, and I felt the need to constantly remind him of that. I often nagged him when he spent time with friends, and always had an attitude about something because of my stubborn personality. And when it was that time of the month and PMS had gotten the best of me, I was rotten to be around.

All I could think about when he died was his last memories of me. I knew how unkind I could be toward someone who had hurt me. Punishing my body with a shortage of food was just another way to deal with my guilt. Just another way to make me suffer, like I had made others suffer with my stubbornness and inability to let go of the past.

My family and closest allies were aware of the bulimia, but no one wanted to talk about it. It was the dirty little secret that became the elephant in the room at family gatherings. It became routine for me to excuse myself to the bathroom after eating. When I'd swallowed the last bite, I made my way to the bathroom and tickled my uvula with the tip of my finger. After a couple months of throwing up, I started to lose my hair from lack of nutrition. It became so thin I would see my scalp every time I pulled it back in a ponytail.

Every day I would step on the scale, watching the number drop with every ounce I regurgitated. As I watched the food particles swirl and disappear down the toilet bowl, I felt like I was flushing away my guilt.

I carried a lot of resentment, and the thought I had been a terrible partner was more than I could handle. I blamed others for things that had nothing to do with the independent choices I had made in the past, which only made me angrier and more estranged from the friends and family who loved me.

So, when the district attorney's office called to suggest restorative justice, I jumped at the idea of dumping everything I was carrying on the driver who had ruined my life, my son's life, and Damin's family and friends. A group of therapists and mediators who were producing a documentary series about the grieving process had created restorative justice. They asked if I'd participate. It was an opportunity for family members of victims to meet face to face with the responsible party before the court date, in hopes of bringing closure to those who were grieving.

The idea of being in a room with him was almost exhilarating. Many times, I had imagined being alone with him and letting my rage run loose like a wild stallion trampling the blue grasses of Kentucky. I needed someone to blame everything on. I couldn't wait to yell and scream at him, telling him how many lives he had ruined with his absence of judgment. How much I hated his very existence!

Amid all my angry thoughts, I realized how many unanswered questions I had and wondered if he had regained his memory. I needed to know if Damin had been asleep. I needed to know why he'd been speeding. I needed to know if Damin had yelled out for him to slow down.

The more I thought about it, I understood that I had to meet him. It was ironic that the man I hated so much might hold the key that might help set parts of my mind free.

After talking with my mom, I called the DA's office back and told them I would speak with him but only if we met at my church. Church was the only place I trusted my ill-tempered behavior. It was the only place I knew I wouldn't attack him. The mediator said he agreed, and restorative justice was in full swing. Before I realized it, the day had arrived.

That morning, when I was driving over to the church, I was so nervous that I was numb. The first participant to arrive, I walked into the silent room on unsteady feet, made my way through the prayer circle of wooden rocking chairs, and anxiously sat down. My small frame shuddered as I gently rocked back and forth, hoping to calm my nerves.

The only thing that eased my worried mind enough to let me keep breathing was the faith that surrounded me. Wooden and ivory crosses hung on the walls, and to the right of the door stood a statue of Mary cradling Jesus. It reminded me we had all been innocent at one point in time. According to the Bible, God had always given us free will . . . free will to love and free will to forgive. I felt shameful sitting there rocking in the house of the Lord with no intentions of doing either.

Praying for my forgiveness, I asked God for closure. I prayed for clarity, and I prayed for the consuming rage that had filled me for so long to leave. I prayed the driver would remember enough to set me free from the questions that haunted me.

Shortly after my lengthy prayer, the woman from restorative justice waltzed in with her expensive leather briefcase and wool clogs. I wondered what I had gotten myself into. Unzipping her Patagonia fleece, she revealed a rose-colored J. Crew blouse she had clearly misbuttoned. I speculated what had led her to work in such an emotionally draining environment, and I debated whether she was strong enough to hold me back if my explosive temper got the best of me.

She sat down in the chair across from me, crossed her legs, and introduced herself. She gently shook my hand and went over some ground rules with me. She assured me that what I was doing showed magnificent strength and bravery, and she concluded her pep talk by telling me that offering forgiveness to those who have caused such pain and torment was a noble thing to do. I told her that forgiveness was far from why I was there and that I had only come to get answers and closure.

This startled her and, not knowing how to respond, she fiddled with her bag, looking for a nonexistent file to fill the uncomfortable silence between us. Hungry as a hawk, I focused on the door, waiting for him to arrive. With my legs tightly crossed at the ankles, I sat quietly in the chair and started counting to one hundred in my head. When I was a teenager, after getting in a fight with a boy at school, I had learned in the anger management group that counting to one hundred helped to slow incipient anger. It also helped with escalating anxiety.

I glanced over to see the mediator with her head buried deep inside her bag. Still counting, I opened my purse and grabbed a small dose of my panic pills. As she searched for her "file," I slipped the calming capsule inside my mouth, allowing my tongue to maneuver it around until it dissolved.

I heard something buzzing far in the distance, and as it grew nearer, I realized it was his motorized wheelchair barreling toward us at full speed. My heart pounded and my body trembled. Suddenly, I felt alive and could sense my blood rushing back through me. I was terrified that I would slip into a panic attack before the meds could fully activate. I began counting faster in my head, anything to make the anxiety go away.

Just as I felt the tingling sensation rising through my body and the tightening of my chest, in he rode with his head down and his tail between his legs. After many weeks, my enemy and I were face to face. I quickly stood up as the mediator moved the rocking chair next to her so he could enter the circle. He spun around and positioned himself diagonally across from me. His body shook with nervousness. He apologized for the jerking and explained that he couldn't control it.

As I stood there staring at him, I noticed his colostomy bag dangling behind the foam cushion he was sitting on. His hair looked greasy, and his baby face was covered with a dingy five o'clock shadow.

He cracked a small smile at me, and I noticed his teeth looked like they hadn't been brushed in weeks. I almost felt sorry for him, but quickly burned away any feelings of pity I had. I reminded myself of all I had suffered on account of *his* recklessness! I pictured De'Andre's devastation the morning I told him his dad wasn't coming home, and I took the image I held of Damin lying unconscious in the hospital bed and placed it in the chair next to me.

The mediator instructed us to speak when we were ready, so I immediately asked him if Damin had been awake at the time of the crash. His eyes grew wide, and his limbs jerked. Feeling like I had upset him, I turned to the mediator for support. Before she could even say anything, he blurted out that he was sorry. He said he was sorry for all the hurt that he caused De'Andre and our family. I asked him again if Damin had been awake. He looked confused and told me he couldn't remember. I felt my blood boil.

He didn't remember. How could he not remember? I burst out that I didn't believe him. He assured me that because of his massive brain injury, he truly didn't know. I quickly told him his injury was nowhere as severe as Damin's. Damin wasn't sitting in a wheelchair; he was at my family's funeral home waiting to be buried when the ground thawed.

As the tension in the room heightened, the mediator explained it was okay for emotions to run high, but that we needed to remember that the accident had affected both parties in different ways. Cutting her off, caring nothing for what she had to say, I asked him about the sweatshirt Damin had been wearing that day.

He allowed his eyes to drift away, unable to look at me, and said he didn't have it. Again, I said I didn't believe him. I told him that Damin wore that sweatshirt every morning and that the paramedics had placed every item they had taken off him in the bag that was returned to me at the hospital. His voice trembled as he insisted he had no recollection of the sweatshirt. I burst into tears.

It was too much. Everything was just too much to absorb. Between the sight of him and his vague answers, I felt even worse. As he watched me cry, he begged me for forgiveness. He told me again how sorry he was and that if he could take Damin's place, he would.

We sat shaking in our chairs until I mustered enough strength to talk. I calmly looked him in the eyes and told him that one day I *might* be able to forgive him, but today was not that day. I told him I was living in hell and my son was suffering as well as Damin's family, and that if I ever reached a point of forgiveness, he would be the first to know but not to hold his breath.

He lowered his head as we both continued to cry together, and at that moment, my enemy and I were the same. We were humans grieving and searching for resolution. I wiped my tears, turned to the mediator, and told her I was finished. Then I walked out the door.

After the meeting, I felt my soul run to a place that was darker than where I had been before. Restorative justice hadn't worked in the way I wanted it to, and in some ways, it made the hostility, guilt, and anger even worse.

I could see that I was falling apart at the seams, and fast. My mother suggested going to a group called Angels' Arms, a bereavement support center for parents and their children. Group sessions consisted of parents meeting in one room and children in the other. They aimed it at bringing people together in moments of tragedy, acting as a support system for those who felt alone. I mainly went for De'Andre, but secretly hoped that it would stop the disturbing thoughts of additional tragedies from creeping in. I also hoped that it would make me stop throwing up everything I ate.

When I first started going, they could see how weak I was. I sat there on the sunken sofa cushion, wanting to fall farther back into the couch, disappearing forever. I remember looking around at everyone and thinking about how much sadness occupied the room.

The room was circular and bordered by heavily used chairs. A small, rectangular table sat in the center of the grief circle with a box of Puffs tissues placed on either end. The oriental rug that I anxiously tapped my feet on, had years of history. The edges were worn and frayed, and it showed evidence of several spills.

At my first meeting, I had to introduce myself and explain why I was there. I made it to "My boyfriend died in a car accident," before bursting into tears and leaving.

As months went on, I grew to learn about the strength that could be gained listening to the adversities of others. I learned there were many kinds of tragedies, and that healing was possible in time. Mostly, they shed few tears and spoke with confidence and clarity as they shared their tragic stories. Their courage inspired me to open up, but I was still too afraid to share the deepest, darkest thoughts I was carrying.

Sometimes I'd be driving down a busy road and I would see a Mac truck coming toward me, and I swear I just wanted to jerk the wheel and smash right into it. I wanted to hear the sounds of the heavy, black metal crumple as it collided with the grill of an eighteen-wheeler. I thought that if I heard what he had heard, maybe it would make the clamorous thoughts in my head die and take my guilt and grief along with them.

I wanted to feel the glass shatter into a million pieces, piercing my body with teeny tiny cuts. I thought if I felt what he had felt, it would all go away. I mean, at the time I thought, *why not? Why not crash head on into a truck and feel nothing, to feel everything?* I would count to ten and hold my breath as the truck flew by me, ignorant of my fantasy.

Angels' Arms seemed to help with the loneliness and feelings that no one else understood, because there, in the large room built for grieving souls, I felt the most normal. It was good for De'Andre too, but by springtime, I had grown so paranoid about death that it took my grief to a whole new level. I couldn't stop perseverating about unexpectedly dying.

I was afraid to tell anyone, as I didn't want them to worry about me. I knew the theories of an untimely death were stemming from grief, but I wasn't ready to talk about them. I wasn't ready to share the swirling emotions of concern I concocted daily.

I imagined every death scenario and placed myself in each one. I was constantly living in fear. The idea of dying petrified me, but I couldn't stop obsessing over all the bad things that might happen to me. I was a horrible person and deserved to be punished by my own torturous thoughts.

I often imagined my funeral and wondered how De'Andre would survive with both of his parents gone. I wanted these sinister thoughts to go away and hoped if I listened to the other group members, that would take my attention off the idea of accidentally dying.

Besides dealing with these strange thoughts, there was a long Maine winter ahead of us, so we had to wait till spring for the burial. Watching the seasons slowly change was depressing. I knew that the ground would soon be soft enough to dig, which was one more thing I preferred to ignore.

Normally, it was a joyous occasion to watch winter winds collide with spring air, conclusively birthing spring into summer, but the thought of having to see everyone again was intimidating. The prospect of reliving emotions similar to those I endured at the funeral was sinking me deeper into the dark place I had yet to get out of. It was like preparing for him to die all over again.

With the burial around the corner, my bulimia and my anxiety about dying had left me on the edge of a slippery slope. To make matters worse, the headstone company I was working with couldn't get the sketch right. Every time they sent their final draft, something was wrong with it. Either the name was misspelled, the picture was in the wrong place, or there was no picture at all. It had me teetering on the verge of a breakdown.

One morning, as I shuffled through the mail, I came across a letter stuck behind a bill. In big, bold italics, plastered in the center of the opaque envelope, was the name of the headstone company. I was eager to see what they had sent and hoped it was finally correct. I grabbed a butter knife to open it and sat down at the kitchen table. I unfolded the paper to reveal what should have been the last sketch of the five-thousand-dollar headstone, but instead turned into the unveiling of my imminent emotional breakdown. The sketch was wrong . . . again. And I lost it!

I realized that yet another mistake meant a whole new drawing needed to be created, possibly pushing us back beyond the deadline for the burial. I ran over to the calendar and confirmed my worst nightmare. There, circled in red pen, was the impending day of closure. There wasn't enough time. How could I possibly bury him with no headstone?

As I stood there staring at the calendar, I was filled with a sudden urge to demolish the company. I wanted to take a sledgehammer and shatter every headstone they had. Unable to prevent the breakdown inching closer by the second, I walked into the bathroom and shut the door. With my back slumped against the washing machine, I sluggishly slid down its metal surface and came to rest on the stained linoleum.

I screamed at the top of my lungs and held my face in my hands as my body rocked back and forth. There on the cold, bathroom floor, I fell into a trance, unable to get out of the black hole I was sliding into. The thoughts that I could no longer ignore were viciously spinning around. All the thoughts I had put on the back burner because I had lawyers to deal with or other painful tasks to complete when someone dies were suddenly swarming around me like bees fleeing a smoke-filled hive. In a matter of moments, I was engulfed by the painful stingers unleashing the emotional demon within.

With the sketch still clutched in my fist, I began ripping it into tiny pieces, as I shouted, "It's wrong, it's wrong, it's wrong!" Then I lunged for the black plastic hangers that dangled inches from my fingertips. I ripped them down off the white wooden bar that sat below my nail polish shelf and screamed louder as each one hit the floor.

Then, as fast as I had thrown them down, I bent over, picked them up off the floor and threw them again but this time at the mirror. Annoyed that the mirror didn't shatter into tiny bits, I quickly turned and faced the pretty nail lacquers that rested neatly organized on the bottom shelf and swept them to the ground.

Metallic nudes and bright florals scattered this way and that. When I ran out of things to throw, I dropped to my knees, faced the wall, and drew back my left fist. With an ear-piercing shriek, I thrust forward a fistful of hate, anger, and guilt. In a full-blown rage on the bathroom floor, I began punching. Repeatedly I punched the grayish wall, waiting to pull back until I heard the thud of my knuckles smacking against the wood.

Each time I yanked my arm back, another thought or memory came forth, releasing it from my mind with a punch of my fist. The nightmares living inside my head were desperate to get out. As I sat on the floor pounding the wall, I watched them escape and explode onto the thick wood before my eyes. I watched my skin burst open across my knuckle bones, spilling blood everywhere. The more I saw, the harder I punched. In my mind, I was bleeding out all the hurt and guilt that had consumed my heart.

I knew that when my outburst was done, pain would rear its ugly head again, but in that moment on the cold linoleum, I felt nothing. After what seemed like an eternity, I paused and stared at the wall. What had once been a beautifully painted bathroom, decorated with quaint knickknacks and pretty nail polish, was transformed into a bloodied canvas of pent-up emotions.

Kicking the crystal colored bottles out of my way, the shards of paper blew backward with the force of my foot. My hand was already swelling, the skin tight and shiny. I had sat there for so long beating the wall that my hand was twice its normal size. I tried bending my thick fingers, but they were stiff as frozen sausage links.

I gasped in horror as I realized what I had just done. How would I explain this to everyone? What would I tell De'Andre? Not knowing if I had broken my hand, I frantically scanned my mind for plausible excuses as I examined my hand change color faster than a clever chameleon. I needed medical attention. Curse words flew out of my mouth left and right as I ran to the car and drove to the hospital.

METAMORPHOSIS

With my good hand on the steering wheel and my mangled hand gently holding a Newport 100, I sucked back the toxic smoke and cursed myself. How could I have been so stupid? Punching the wall had solved nothing. The headstone was still incorrect, and the burial was still going to happen whether or not I wanted it to. The only difference was that I might have broken my hand.

As I spun the leather wheel left and then right, I tried coming up with different scenarios for my ballooned hand. Anything was better than the truth. So, I decided I would lie and tell everyone the window fell on it while I was installing an air conditioner.

Somewhat content with my fib, I took my injured hand away from the cigarette in my mouth and let it dangle loosely from my lips. I felt sick to my stomach thinking I would have to lie about how I'd gotten my injury. It didn't really help me elude the shame and embarrassment of my self-abuse.

With all senses on high alert, I listened to the pulse in my hand. I held it high above my head to elevate the throbbing mass. *Thump-thump*, my hand sang loudly in the air. I was overwhelmed and frustrated, but my pain was a potent reminder of life. Somewhere deep down inside my broken self, I had been alive enough to lose my sanity in the comfort of my home. Everyone had their moments of weakness when dealing with grief, and the bathroom episode had been mine.

Tears formed as I pulled into the parking lot. I was only human, but I had let my anger and emotions get the best of me. I needed more time to be healed and to have closure. Whether it was court, burial issues, or grief, I had to find better ways to deal with the pressure than punching household walls or purposely vomiting.

My reflection in the rearview mirror was ghastly. I licked my pointer finger and wiped the dried, crusted tears from my cheekbones. With my lips now wrapped tightly around my cigarette, I took one last drag before tossing it. I got out of the car and, with my shoes planted firmly on the ground, I walked toward the front entrance.

Like a recording, I went over my fabricated story in my head again and again. Was it believable? Maybe, but what mattered most in that moment was that I recognized I had just survived my first breakdown and I was okay. I understood that if I was going to make it through future hurdles, I needed to reevaluate how I would release the anger when it arrived. Punching a pillow seemed preferable to punching the wall.

With my head held high, I took the last few steps of my walk of shame. I walked through the automatic doors, approached the desk, and checked myself in.

The Burial

When I woke up that June morning, the day of the burial, I knew what lay ahead of me held. During the months leading up to that Saturday, I had wanted nothing to do with it, but when I awoke that morning, something inside me seemed different. I was ready to lay him to rest and begin searching for the peace I desperately needed. I was ready for the tears to stop. I had cried every day since he died, so much that I had developed chronic dry eye. The optometrist told me I literally had cried my eyes dry.

After waking up, I gobbled down a breakfast that was fit for Tiffany's . . . a double dose of meds washed down with cold coffee, which had become my normal breakfast routine. I nibbled on a few bites of burnt toast and remembered to take my Tums along with it. Often nauseated by my anxiety, I needed something to help settle my stomach most mornings. Incorporating the chalky, chewable morsels into my daily routine helped quell the roaring dragon inside my stomach.

After eating, I took extra time getting ready. Since I was nursing a badly injured hand, doing my hair and applying makeup was a painstaking slow process, thanks to the bulky, fiberglass cast held in place with a now dingy Ace bandage.

Amazed that my hand was not broken, the doctors thought immobilizing it for two weeks was the best way to treat it. The swelling was severe, and since I couldn't bend my fingers, they felt it was best to let it heal with as little movement as possible. I lived alone and was concerned about the limitations of a permanent cast. I begged them to fit me with a removable one and gave my Girl Scout's honor to wear it constantly.

I now turned my attention to the dress hanging from the rusted curtain rod, wondering if I would ever one day learn how to iron. I had successfully pleaded with my mother to press the wrinkles from the short, pleated dress, which she had placed high on the curtain rod to prevent any further creasing.

As I stood in front of the open window, I closed my eyes and let the warm breeze that drifted in brush against my skin. It felt like a warm embrace, but I realized that the two little pills I had swallowed for breakfast were most likely causing the warmth. I smiled anyway and opened my eyes. The wind gently rattled the shade, making the bottom of my dress dance. The frolicking fabric mesmerized me and as I stepped closer to let the hem flutter against my fingertips. It was then, looking out the window, I saw a cluster of bluebirds sitting on a tree branch up ahead.

A sign in our family of a message sent from above, the colorful blue feathers and plump white bellies that visited me that morning brought a smile to my face. I knew I wasn't alone.

Our arrival at the cemetery a couple of hours later brought mixed emotions. The gravel made a crunching sound as it wedged between the grooves of the tires. Each rotation made my stomach churn, as it brought me that much closer to his gravesite.

We traveled down the narrow pathway, my mother, De'Andre, and I, in silence. The thousands of souls laid to rest were a reality check as to where we were and what we were about to do. Hours earlier, I had felt ready and prepared, but as we pulled up and looked at the fresh dirt and the finished headstone, it filled me with sorrow.

The headstone company, embarrassed by how many times it had taken to get the sketch right, had worked overtime to have it ready for the service. I was grateful for their accomplishment, which only furthered my own embarrassment about the tantrum I had thrown when I thought it wouldn't be ready.

I watched from the car as our friends, family, and Damin's coworkers showed up months after the accident in support. It was moving and spoke volumes about how many lives he had touched. As everyone circled around the grave, I was more than ready to start, but didn't want to proceed until everyone had arrived.

After surveying the group, I noticed that one particular person was missing. Standing tall at six foot five and weighing in at close to three hundred pounds, Todd wasn't easily missed, even in a crowd of mourners. I made my way around the circle, asking our closest friends if they had seen or heard from him. It was strange he hadn't arrived yet. He was Damin's best friend, as well as my friend and an honorary uncle to De'Andre. It annoyed me that he was running late, and after multiple phone calls to his cell went unanswered, I had to decide whether to wait or start without him.

As I surveyed the crowd of mourners, I could tell that they had waited long enough. Having to bury him months later was an emotional mind fuck, and I knew that those who had come wanted it over just as much as I did.

The priest informed me he couldn't wait any longer, so I gave him the okay to start. I turned to a small group of friends and cursed Todd for not being there. Throughout the service, I continued to peer over my shoulder looking for his imposing stature, but he never showed. During the priest's closing words, all I could focus on was the fact that Todd wasn't there. The prayers everyone muttered in unison under their breath were like a silent rebuke. I couldn't stop perseverating on his absence and the fact that he had never contacted me.

I could feel the tears welling up behind my black Ray Bans. Not wanting to show signs of weakness, I dug my nails into the back of my leg as a counterirritant, warding off my tears. A lump sat heavy in my throat as I spoke up and invited everyone to the celebration of life I had put together at Damin's favorite pub.

As people climbed into their cars, I noticed some of my friends stationed just beneath the willow tree. I ran over to talk to them before catching a ride with my mother. Foaming at the mouth like Cujo, I vented about Todd and said he "better be fucking dead" to not have shown up today. We all stood there in disbelief and tried making sense of his silence. Something was undoubtedly wrong.

I couldn't get to the pub fast enough. As soon as my mother put her Toyota Corolla in park, I raced through the doors and made a beeline for the bar. I firmly asked for a double shot of Patrón with no chaser, and covertly slipped my second dose of meds under my tongue. After tossing back the tequila, just as I had at the funeral, I wiped the corners of my mouth with my sleeve. The burn of the alcohol tickled my throat as I swallowed hard and went to greet the arriving guests.

As I made my rounds after everyone had piled in, I could hear the whispers circulating about Todd's mysterious absence. I was pissed. Instead of people reflecting on Damin's accomplishments, Todd's whereabouts were the focus. The consensus seemed to be that he was probably passed out in bed, unable to hear his alarm clock going off.

The more I heard, the angrier I became. I was going to kill him when I finally saw him. Taking a much-needed break, I headed outside to the deck to get some fresh air. I pulled out a cigarette from my pack and lit it. Deep in thought, I wondered how, at age twenty-eight, I had planned a wake, a funeral, a burial, and now a celebration of life. It was a lot to wrap my head around.

Bold smoke rings leaked from the end of my poison stick with every drag I took. The coolness of the menthol was soothing. I wondered, as I watched the outline of the O-shaped fumes disappear, if Damin would be proud of me for what I had accomplished. In a few hours, everything would be over. I stubbed out my Newport Long and returned to the celebration. My dress shoes clicked across the wooden floor as I waltzed over to the bar and ordered another double.

It all felt like a dream, drinking and watching everyone around me. Because of the relaxing power of my afternoon pills in combination with the alcohol, I felt once again like I was out of my body. Like a robot, I nodded my head to any question, and as the afternoon grew old, I an overwhelming sense of relief began to filter in. Only a matter of minutes stood between me and an empty house where I could be alone, away from everyone. I could endure whatever emotion I was feeling without having to put on a brave face, smile, and answer inane questions.

Although I'd already exceeded my alcohol-to-pill ratio, I bothered the bartender for one more shot before closing out the tab. The room was filled with people, but I only saw the picture display tables of Damin and others. Slowly, I circled the tables and took one last view of the memories there. I couldn't help but smile remembering happier times until I came across a photo of Todd and Damin together, frozen in time. I clutched the metal frame in my hand and wondered where the hell Todd was. Hurt and angry, I set the photo back down. I said my goodbyes, thanked everyone for coming, and left.

When my mother and I finally pulled into her driveway after the celebration, I felt free, free from having to set aside any more time to deal with death. For the first time in months, I didn't have to think about flowers, headstones, or cemetery plot prices. As I stepped out of the car, I planted my foot root firmly into the ground. I felt sturdy, like the tall pines that filled Maine's dense forests. I wasn't weighed down by the impending burial anymore.

My feet firm on the pavement, I walked across the driveway and into my mother's house. I tossed my cell phone on the table and collapsed on the hand-me-down couch that sat kitty-corner in her living room. I sighed deeply and closed my eyes, imagining what the rest of my summer would be like. It was strange to feel free from the diligent task of funeral planning, but at the same time, I didn't know what I would do now to fill my days. I had been absorbed with making everything perfect for Damin. Now, I had nothing to fill the empty hours, nothing to keep me from accepting reality.

Before my mind could spin out of control, thinking of all the ways I could keep busy, I heard my phone vibrating on the glass table. Jumping up, I scurried over to answer it. In bold, bubble letters, Christina's name flashed on the screen. I slid my thumb across the fingerprinted glass to answer. Before she could even get out a hello, I cut her off immediately and said I was okay. I told her she didn't need to worry about me, but before I could tell her any more, I heard her whimper.

I asked her what was happening. She ignored my question and asked me where I was. Confused, I hesitantly told her I was at my mother's. She advised me to go outside. Afraid that someone had complained about how I had arranged the burial or the celebration, I did as she asked. If that were the case, I didn't want my mother or De'Andre to hear me get upset.

I stood beside the outdoor table and traced my fingers along the tattooed pattern engraved in the plastic, trying to calm my nerves, impatient to find out what was going on. With a trembling voice, Christina said that she'd had a call from Todd's mother. He wasn't at the burial because he was dead. Died. Never woke up in the morning. His mother had waited to tell us because she didn't want to take away from Damin's burial. She was so selfless, faced with the loss of her own son, that she put her grieving on hold and waited before notifying his closest friends.

I felt a familiar tingle start up my legs and run down to the depths of my stomach. Like a boat caught in a perfect storm, the tingling sensation tumbled about in waves of tequila acid before moving on to my heart. Squeezing it tightly like a fist draining the juice of a lemon, the tingles of shock continued upward before they arrived in my brain. I could feel hot tears dripping from my eyes. My whole body felt engulfed in flames. I exploded, sending flashes of rage everywhere.

I threw my phone on the ground, reached for the table, lifted it up with both hands, and hurled it at the shed. Shards of plastic flew in the air like turkey feathers during hunting season and began dodging plastic bullets as they sailed backward toward me. I scooped up the dislocated table leg and began beating it against the wooden panels of the shed, screaming at the top of my lungs. Like my tantrum on the bathroom floor, I bashed the plastic limb against the cream-colored shed until I was left holding only a small, six-inch stub.

My mother flew out through the screen door, begging me to stop. She reached for the phone and picked it up off the freshly cut lawn. Her voice stern, she yelled into the phone and was greeted with the same devastating news. I listened to her gasp and cry for God's mercy.

I fell to my knees and begged for forgiveness for the many times I had cursed him that day, for saying that he "better be fucking dead." Memories sped through my mind unbidden. How could he possibly be dead? How could he die the same day we buried Damin? Trying to understand was pointless. I would never know why. Wiping the tears from my swollen eyes, I calmly walked over to my mother's car. All the life was sucked out of me in that moment. My heart was bitter. I reached in to grab my pack of cigarettes and then stared at my mother. De'Andre's small face peeked out from behind the screen door, wondering what all the commotion was about. I steadily lit my cigarette and inhaled deeply. I hated life, myself, and the hole I was about to fall deeper into as I blew the smoke out and turned my back on my family.

Down the Rabbit Hole

The double dose of death so close together had me at my wits end. Like a forest fire started deep within the woods, I watched as the flames moved briskly outward extending past any edge of reason I had left. Nothing seemed real anymore, and soon everything started coming undone. The bulimia grew worse and so did my benzodiazepine intake. Although the little white pills were aimed at treating anxiety, they treated an array of other symptoms including insomnia, seizures, and depression, as well as for sedation before surgery. The catalog of side effects that came along with it basically made the wonder pill break even. Although the benzos had kept me functioning, after several months, they were wreaking havoc on my body.

My hair was becoming much thinner, and when I did shower, clumps of tangled curls would be woven through my skinny fingers. I'd let the warm water fall on the loose strands intertwined between my knuckles, and watch it collect at the drain.

If shedding more hair wasn't embarrassing enough, I began to get the shakes so bad that I struggled to cut my food when I pretended to eat in front of people. I would timidly look around at the dinner table to see if my mother or grandmother would notice the quivering utensils in my hand. I knew they were aware of the eating disorder, which almost made throwing up around them less humiliating, but I wondered if they saw me struggle with my fork as I forced the unwanted food into my mouth.

One of the worst things about pretending to eat and using benzos was the accompanying dry mouth. It felt like a vacuum had sucked out all my saliva, making it impossible to chew and swallow. Every bite of food I ate tasted like a mixture of saltines and my grandmother's day-old Southern cornbread. It was annoying and taxing on the jaw.

Not fully caring to understand all the side effects and willing to deal with the ones I had, I continued popping benzos like Tic-Tacs. They were my superheroes when fear threatened to take over. As soon as I would feel my heart race and my body tingle, I knew the impending panic attack would soon paralyze me. The attacks could last for several minutes, hours, sometimes days. I would get so fixated on whatever unthinkable thing that might happen next, it became hard to leave the house.

If I got into the truck to drive somewhere, I thought for sure I would be in an accident. Quick trips weren't any easier. Most mornings, I could barely get into my vehicle and drive down the road to bring De'Andre to school. I couldn't let him take the bus; that was even more dangerous. What if it tipped over going around a sharp corner? What if the bus lost its brakes, plummeting into a ditch, or even worse, the river?

As time pressed on, I wondered if I would eventually get to a point where I was unable to leave my confining walls of protection. But somehow, I could still concoct some strange scenario of how I could get hurt in my home. I felt so sorry for what my life was turning into, but I couldn't help focusing on all the other things that could go wrong after everything bad that had already happened. In my mind, it seemed as though I was being punished for all the awful things I had done and said to other people.

Existing in such negativity day in and day out was turning me into a different person. My soul was becoming black, like my thoughts. My touch was colder, far more distant than it used to be. I was growing absent as a mother, and whenever I tried looking at my reflection in a mirror, a stranger stared back at me, a stranger with eyes as lifeless as a stuffed deer's head. My heart had grown hard, and my ability to appreciate each sunrise had vanished. I looked frail and brittle, identical to the walking dead.

About a year after the accident, I had wasted away to practically nothing. I began drinking Ensure shakes the physician had recommended to gain weight, but they tasted like shit and had me feeling as if I belonged in the geriatric unit. I was supposed to drink three a day, but on a good day I could choke down one. Of course, I hadn't told the doctor the real reason for my extreme weight loss, plummeting to 112 pounds at five foot five, but I gave the calorific, lactose-free shakes a shot and drank as much as I could. I had nothing left to lose except my love for dairy-free products and my last ounces of sanity.

Without having to be told, I realized I was getting worse. Down the rabbit hole I went a little more each day, sinking like Alice into a dreamworld that led to my own hellish wonderland. To add more fuel to the fire, the pills were slowly losing their potency, and the only way to feel any sort of relief was to take more. This allowed my limp fingers to claw at the tunnel around me hoping to slow my fall.

Increasing my dose of meds also detached me further from reality. I began floating into another world, moving like a lost object through space. I cut off all contact with anyone close to me. It was safer that way. If I was alone, losing someone else wouldn't hurt me. No one else could cause me pain.

Even though my self-inflicted hibernation was intended to protect me, I was still lonely. I had never lived alone, and it was hard to face adult responsibilities on my own. It was a true testament of strength and weakness colliding, waiting to see which one would come out on top. There were days where I wanted to be strong for De'Andre, but the terror was too debilitating. I felt frozen, frightened with every step I took. I had finally reached bottom.

My mother often tried to help me to see the many blessings I still had, but I was too far gone. I was living in a world of grayness and gloom. The obscurity of my domain had become so severe I was blind to the shadow of my son lurking behind me in need of love and attention. Thankfully, her strong, motherly love helped make up emotionally for what I couldn't do for De'Andre. She provided a piece of parenting I couldn't seem to fit into the family puzzle. My aunt and grandmother were a huge help too, supporting De'Andre in any way they could.

My loss of parental skills made my feelings of guilt overwhelming. It had been well over the timeframe when most grieving parents would have bucked up, but I couldn't pull things together. I didn't want to fail as a parent when my child needed me most, but I didn't know how to fix it or how to fix myself. I didn't know how to get to a place where I could be neutral.

I knew that grieving was an important process, but the state I was in felt like so much more. Inside I wasn't normal. I felt inhuman, unable to feel anything, and at the same time feeling every single thought my crazed mind was generating.

Living in the inner sanitorium I had created had become almost normal in my eyes. Using what had happened as a crutch to validate my personal madness made it that much easier to tolerate. It was my new destiny; my calling to live out the daily nightmares in my head.

As soon as my eyes opened, I was met with obsessive prospects of how I might die or get hurt that day. They were so expected and had become part of my daily survival that in some sick way, I looked forward to topping the thoughts from the day before.

I was accustomed to the prison I had crafted. I was a professional "anxietist," and nothing was going to take that away from me.

Mirror, Mirror

Two years after the accident, my determination to find something wrong with my body was at its peak. I had also started drinking again. I had gotten to a better place as far as parenting, bulimia, and getting out more. I had taken up exercise as an outlet, leaving most of my bad habits behind because of it, but the phobias of accidental bodily harm persisted.

To counteract the feelings, I began having a small glass of wine before bed. In the beginning, I never had more than one because after a couple years of negative thoughts, it petrified me to have some sort of reaction to the pills I was still taking. Every time I drank, I'd imagined De'Andre finding me dead the next morning in bed because I had consumed a lethal combination of prescription pills and alcohol. Even though I had done so during the funeral and burial celebration, the fear of double dipping never registered until later.

My paranoid thoughts about disease and death were increasing each day, and the wine wasn't helping. I exchanged one bad habit for another, fixating on all the terrible tragedies that could happen to me during the day and drowning them out with wine at night.

Before I knew it, my nightly glass of wine had multiplied. Filled with empty bottles, my storage closet turned into a wine cellar. The thick, glass bottles were piled up so high that I couldn't see the dirty floor they covered. To make matters worse, I was showing up to work hungover, completely functional, but hungover.

Drinking on school nights made the constant swearing by the children the following morning that much harder not to swear back at them. As a school-based behavioral health professional, they had trained me to not engage in petty behavior with a minor refusing to do their schoolwork. But I would come into work with the previous night's pinot on my breath, angry at the world, which left me hating my job and annoyed with the behavioral students I was working with.

My mind was spinning out of control with all the possible ailments that could dominate me, and I couldn't take it anymore! I went so far as to cut what I thought was a wart seedling out of various places on my fingers, thinking they would consume my whole body if I didn't.

Every time I saw what looked like a black, speckled dot near the surface of my skin, I would perform minor surgery in my upstairs bathroom. The lighting was the best in there. I would thoroughly cleanse my hands, followed by saturating the entire area with alcohol and just when I thought I had sterilized enough, I disinfected twice more.

With the sterile cuticle clippers my mother had given me for Christmas years ago, I would cut away at the coarse skin that stood between the snippers and what I considered a wart virus. A quick snip here and a quick snip there, I was saving a trip to the doctor. I didn't need a physician to tell me I was hindering a wart in progress. I had a doctorate in mental dysfunction and discovering potential bodily illness. I knew what I was doing, or at least I thought I did.

As I watched the stainless steel cut into my finger, I wondered how on earth I would ever be normal again. Every day I was battling a new disorder. I was my own worst enemy. I had so much free time on my hands, I started creating novels in my head of all the things that could go wrong in my life. The trauma from the accident was brewing a deadly batch of poison in my brain, and each thought only added more fuel to the fire.

The intrusive thoughts were like ocean waves crashing upon shore. One right after the other, flooding the beaches of my mind, drawing back a piece of my sanity as it disappeared into the water like footprints left in sand.

Like a thief in the night stealing what strength I had gained, I wondered how many others had fallen victim like myself? How many others had gotten sucked into the undertow of paranoia and destructive thinking? Inside my mind, I was clawing at the walls to get out.

Even when I attempted to run, something would always suck me back in. As if the intrusive, personal thoughts of self-destruction weren't enough, I began fearing everyone around me. The gentleman coughing in front of me at the grocery store was probably carrying influenza. Surely, I would get it if I inhaled the air he was breathing. The woman whose hands were grubby like a young boy's were most likely carrying some type of disease. How could I possibly grab the door handle after she touched it? And it didn't stop there. Even stopping at red lights, I would glance over to see people staring at me and thought they would follow me home and hurt me.

I couldn't go anywhere or do anything without somehow incorporating fear of harm into it. I was a magnet for tragic situations, so why wouldn't something else unthinkable happen to me? I was manifesting all the horrible things I could imagine. When people tell you to think positive in every situation, I was just the opposite. It didn't feel right unless I was prepping for another lousy day at the office. If I were prepared, it would somehow make the pain less excruciating when it finally arrived.

So every night I would drink until I passed out. I would drink and dance in my kitchen alone until I had danced so much I was dizzy. I had traded an eating disorder for alcoholism and traded tears of grief for orchestrating potential health catastrophes.

My concerns about cancer, skin disease, car accidents, stalking, house fires, heart attacks, angina, gum disease, and more flooded my head daily. At night, I checked my door incessantly to make sure it was locked before I went to bed. Every time I lit my favorite candle, I'd quadruple check to make sure that the blown-out flame was "really out," even though I had watched its glowing fire diminish to a charred wick with my own two eyes.

My mind was a spinning game show wheel. Every section it landed on was a winner, and my wheel of wonders offered prizes of insanity and paranoia. I couldn't get through my day without envisioning being harmed in some way. I would spend all day trying to plan how I could prevent the fabricated disasters. I was so fucked up that I couldn't even begin to comprehend the level of grief I was experiencing, and the alcohol only made it worse.

The turning point was when I had my last episode on the bathroom floor. I scratched my back and felt something round protruding slightly above my right shoulder blade. At first, I thought it was a pimple or a bite of some sort, so I walked into the downstairs bathroom to investigate. I angled my body just right and turned my head back as far as it would go. I was relieved to find that the tiny bump was nothing more than a pimple. Then I noticed a small amount of discoloration just above it.

I began tracing the light-colored skin expecting it to end just as soon as I had found it, but it didn't. Farther and farther up it went. Around my neck and down the left side of my shoulder it traveled. By the time I had traced the discolored pattern, it seemed like the state of Texas had been drawn on my back and shaded in with a pale-colored pencil.

I felt my heart start to race and panic set in. What was this pale color that had taken over my beautiful mocha skin? Immediately, only one plausible explanation came to mind. I had somehow developed vitiligo, and it was only a matter of time before it spread all over my body. How could anyone love me now? How would I cope? I had been dark skinned my whole life. As a child I dreamed of being covered in creamy beige-colored skin, but not like this. I wanted my brown skin. I wanted all of it.

I started to hyperventilate. My toes became tingly, and the sensation moved up my body and rested in my arms. My chest became tight as I struggled to breathe. I put my hand on the sink to prevent me from falling as my knees weakened, wobbling in terror. I slowly bent down to sit on the toilet, ripped off my pants, and meticulously examined my lower extremities. I found areas on my legs that looked similar, but not as severe. Convinced that I did indeed have vitiligo, I fell to the floor and screamed. With De'Andre at after-school care, I willingly gave in to my terror.

Tears flowed heavily from my eyes while I shouted for someone to help me, but no one came. I was alone. The house was empty; its only occupants were my crazed self and my new skin disease. There I lay, curled in a ball on the cold floor, trying to rock my mind into a calmer state.

After fifteen minutes had passed, I dragged my limp body partially up and leaned my back against the wall. There I sat, contemplating what had just happened. I understood I hadn't received a medical diagnosis of vitiligo and needed to think of other things that could be responsible. However, the more I tried, the more I thought about how the disease would continue to spread before eventually taking over my entire body.

I abruptly stood up and faced the vanity, hoping to snap the unruly image from my mind. Once again, my reflection in the mirror was unrecognizable. On the outside, I looked sane and put together; on the inside, I was screaming for help. Worry was slowly killing what was left of my competency. I knew I needed to get my head right and was well aware that I couldn't do it alone. So, I went to the doctor to be examined and to see how I would treat my self-diagnosed vitiligo.

The disposable paper crumpled beneath me as I squirmed on the examination table. His breath was heavy and fingers rough as he traced the outline of my fictitious disease. As I waited for his confirmation, expecting him to tell me I had months before the skin condition fully consumed my petite frame, he sat down on his stool and pushed his glasses on top of his head. A strange look appeared on his face. My stomach plummeted waiting for him to speak. He looked up, placed his hand on mine, and told me I could cure my dry skin with a thick moisturizer and less frequent showers.

I felt sick to my stomach and immediately asked him to refer me to a psychologist. When I got home, I dumped out every ounce of alcohol I had. The trauma from Damin and Todd unexpectedly dying so close together had turned me into a head case. The only thing I thought could save me was a good head doctor.

Therapy

Shortly after my first appointment, they diagnosed me with a high level of PTSD, anxiety, and insomnia. They talked me into changing my meds and put me on a new cocktail of pharmaceuticals: a daily anxiety med, an emergency anxiety med, sleeping pills, and blood pressure meds to help keep my constant nightmares at bay.

I left the office a mess. I wondered how things had gotten so bad so quickly. I hated the idea of the medication and vowed to get off everything one day. The doctor assured me I could, with weekly cognitive therapy sessions and provided I took my meds now as directed. I didn't want to commit to either, but felt I had no choice. I wanted to be well again. I was at rock bottom, so I accepted the advice of medical professionals and committed to the treatment.

Within a few short weeks into therapy, I started seeing a difference. I began sleeping better, which helped me to feel well in the morning. The pills knocked me out for at least five hours, allowing my mind to rest properly. In addition to sleeping soundly, the bad dreams subsided. Before, I had often dreamt of being chased, kidnapped, shot, raped, choked, stabbed, and fiercely being hurled about in tornadoes.

The tornado dreams were the most frequent. I'll never forget the sounds of the whipping winds screaming like witches, tossing me like a child's ball. Around and around I went, waiting to fall or be flung into something, knocking me awake. I would pray in my dreams to wake up, and when I finally did, I would be terrified and drenched in sweat. I would lie there alone in my bed, too frightened to move. Eventually, I would have to, so I could change and grab a dry blanket to cover my shivering body.

I soon noticed that my thoughts were becoming less intrusive most days, and if they showed their angry face, I used my therapy skills to keep them at bay. Before I'd work my way into a frenzy, I'd examine the evidence at hand. Where was the proof? Was I jumping to conclusions?

Running through the steps of thinking before reacting was helping in difficult situations. However, sometimes what I'd learned failed to serve me in the way I needed it to. Like the day I chased my mother down the hall at work begging her to examine my gums. Two minutes earlier, I had given myself a dental examination in the poorly lit bathroom.

My mother and I worked together at a public school, which was a blessing for me and a curse for her. Too often, I would run down to her office, nervous about another negative thought I had developed during my fifteen-minute break. On most occasions, between the therapy technique, properly dosed meds, and my mother talking me off the edge, I could walk out of her tiny classroom reassured, but not on the day of my oral exam. This particular paranoid thought was a force to be reckoned with.

I begged her to look at my gums. She quickly assured me she didn't need to look, that my gums were fine, and I was only doing "that thing" I did. I felt both insulted and somewhat reassured by her comment, but still, I needed validation.

She insisted she wasn't a dentist and suggested that, because my skin was darker, perhaps my gums would be too. But when I burst into tears right there in the hallway, she whispered for me to open my mouth. Her blue eyes widened with determination and darted back and forth as she peered in. She pulled away momentarily to see if anyone was coming, and then looked once more and told me I appeared perfectly healthy.

I took a step back, leaned against the painted, cinder-block wall, and broke down, knowing that I had once again wasted her time and mine. I wiped away my tears of embarrassment and gratefully thanked her before heading back to the breakroom to pull myself together.

On that day, I fully understood the severity of my instability. I knew the meds were a crutch, and once they wore off, I was in serious trouble. I knew that one day, the definition of the successful healing I wanted to encompass was an empty medicine cabinet in my upstairs bathroom and pleasant morning breaks with my mother.

Though I hated the trauma that was trying to define me, I refused to give up. Some days I would leave therapy exhausted. I scheduled my appointments after work, so by the time I got home, it was time to start dinner. Between work and stabilizing my mental health, I was rundown and emotionally drained. Still, I kept going every week. Even when the tears came or the panic attacks surfaced, every Tuesday at three o'clock, I sat on the blue leather sofa and revisited the old trauma.

Years later, with a trio of psychologists under my belt and enough prescriptions to open a pharmacy, I still wasn't better in how I hoped I would be after being in therapy for so long. I was much further along than when I started, but I continued to depend on medication. The scripts were still getting filled, but not as much. Then, one weekend in June 2017, everything changed once again.

My close friend—the one who watched De'Andre the night of the accident—was in town for her first visit back after moving out of state. We spent the weekend at my house, drinking margaritas and eating cheap Mexican food, which was exactly what I needed to get back on track. Saturday night, she wanted to go out and escape for an evening. I declined a road trip to Portland, but promised we would visit some local bars.

I despised going out. There was no point. Everyone I ran into was the same, drunk and looking to have fun, and I had no interest in either. So we set out with no expectations. We sipped our tequila on the rocks and chatted about life and how teachers and techs were underpaid, underappreciated, and always got the short end of the stick.

I never fully grasped the challenges of teaching or "tech-ing" until I started working at the school. My first year at the Park School, I broke my pinky finger and had to wear a removable cast for six months. While attempting to restrain a student who was out of control (a common safety practice with violent, autistic children), my partner had shut the door while my finger was still in it. Unfortunately, I yanked upward after feeling the pinch, ripping off my nail and breaking the tiny extremity. After that experience, I had a newfound respect for those working in special ed!

We took a break from sipping our drinks and made our way outside. I couldn't light my cigarette fast enough. Inhaling deeply, I watched as people passed in their summer clothes. Cargo shorts and flip-flops adorned every male who walked by. Their baby faces, covered with sparse hair, told the story of their youth and inexperience. I listened to their sandals slap loudly against the pavement as they announced how many shots they had taken at the bar. We laughed at their blatant attempts to impress us with their drinking skills and then turned to discuss what boring bar we'd try next.

It was Waterville, Maine, and our four choices were far from enticing. It was too early to leave, but the night felt like a waste. We decided to make the most of our evening and opted for a quick selfie before venturing onwards. With our backs to the parking lot, we faced inward with our knees bent and attempted to capture the moment but were unsatisfied with the results. So we asked two young girls walking by if they could kick our photo session up a notch and snap the picture for us. They were delighted to help and instructed us to move closer to the light. We stood with our arms around each other, staring into my iPhone.

With the help of our nameless photographers, we changed positions with every frame, maximizing our mini photo shoot. After close to a minute, the kind girls walked over and passed me back my phone. The two of us, eager to see what they had captured, ran over to the lamppost and reviewed them.

We were happy with what we saw and screamed out with excitement at the "postable" social media pics the girls had taken of us. As my fingers swiped through the photos, we blurted out "That one's really good!" And that's when it happened.

A strong masculine voice from behind said, "Yeah, it is!" I whipped my head around to see whose voice responded to our shout-out, and when I did, I stood there like a deer in the headlights, not believing what I was feeling.

There, in the shadows of the night, the stars and the Universe aligned. In a matter of seconds, I could feel my stomach filling with butterflies. I lost myself in the sea-blue irises that stared back at me and felt my heart quiver and my palms get sweaty as he smiled.

He stood tall with his strong build, his fitted Nike tee stretched over his taut body. The retro Jordan sneakers he wore were a pleasant surprise from the flip-flops that had sung loudly in my ear just moments before. He stepped closer to me and said he knew who I was. His fingers reached for my sweaty hand as he explained it had been a long, long time ago when we met, and that even though I might not remember him, he surely remembered me.

I asked him what my name was. I prayed that the stranger in the night I had just met wasn't attempting a trite pickup line. I held my breath while I waited for his response: "Ashley." My mouth fell open as destiny circled around us and fate spun its web. He explained we had met at a party almost seventeen years before. I couldn't believe it. How could he remember me after that long?

He joined my friend and me for the rest of our outing, and as the night went on, it seemed as if we had known one another for years.

As the clock approached one, we danced to the closing song that played in the small basement of a local bar, a remix of Oasis's "Wonder Wall" blending with the brash voices and heavy feet occupying the dance floor. He pulled me in closer, lifted me up off my feet, and held me close as I wrapped my legs around him.

We looked into each other's eyes, and he kissed me. I kissed him back and held on tightly. As the dim lights slowly brightened, he gently placed me back down, took my hand, and led me outside to a waiting taxi.

In that moment, I did not know that he and I would become inseparable from that day on. I hadn't the slightest clue what the Universe had in store for us, but in that exact place in time, I knew he was supposed to be a part of my life. Within a month, C.J. had helped me gain strength in ways I didn't think were possible.

He pushed me to see that I had been using what had happened as an excuse to become dependent on medication. Within months of meeting him, I was completely off my meds. And four months into our relationship, I was pregnant... unexpectedly. I had become the small percent of women who got pregnant on the pill.

I continued with therapy during pregnancy. I worked hard at leaving my old ways behind and did the best I could with the raging surge of hormones that rushed through me. I was happy to be medication free and felt healthy and natural, making for a wonderful pregnancy.

When the baby finally came, we were thrilled. Even De'Andre was pumped to be a big brother. After Amaya's birth, I was still off the medication, with no intention of ever going back on. I kept my weekly appointments with my therapist, bringing her with me. She slept the whole time, allowing me to talk and listen without interruption.

It felt good to be med-free, and for so long, and it felt good to start a fresh chapter in my life. But no matter how hard I tried, the anxious thoughts still made their presence known from time to time: illnesses, accidents. I couldn't escape them, even with years of treatment on my resume.

This time around, I had dreamed up exciting new things to worry about, including a phobia of food poisoning, and I constantly checked the "use by" dates and compulsively smelled every meat, poultry, or fish product I used. I was concerned about items properly being stored and baked and was driving my family nuts every time they cooked for me, asking if they had cooked the food to the appropriate temperature. I was obsessed with letting everything cool before storing it in the fridge to avoid the growth of bacteria. In addition, I worried about product tampering and checked for broken seals . . . constantly. I even returned two tubes of toothpaste to CVS after seeing that there was no foil seal glued to the end of the tube. By the third tube, I realized that there was no foil seal on this brand, only in my mind.

There was something the doctors were missing, and about a month before my thirty-fourth birthday, fed up with my lack of improvement, I quit therapy. Weeks later, my dear friend changed my life, opening my eyes to something new.

Section Two

Transformation

Eleven days after my thirty-fourth birthday, I walked past a book suggested by a dear friend of mine as it sat comfortably alone on my staircase. Pausing, examining the accumulating dust bunnies hovering over the book jacket, I wondered what the big secret was? What was so special about it?

I bent over, clutching the small book in my hand, and began eyeing its unique cover. With a scripture-like scroll wrapped around the front and a ruby red, wax stamp leaving a signature seal at the top, the book looked more like a secret map. The kind of map you'd see in pirate movies that led to precious jewels buried deep inside a cave on Treasure Island.

Flipping it over to view the backside, I questioned whether the book really held the key to what I was looking for as promised. I also wondered if I could actually find time to read any book from cover to cover. Never a reader and always a writer, I contemplated what I would be getting into as I stood quietly on the bottom step.

I quickly scanned the last six months in my mind and reminded myself what had led me to the book in the first place. If I really wanted to find the time to read it, I would. Fanning its pages like a flipbook between my fingers, glancing at its intimidating word count, I remembered a key piece of advice a coworker had given me years ago when I had first started writing with the goal of publication: "If you want to become a better writer, read."

I allowed his words of wisdom to trickle in at the very moment I needed them. If the book failed me miserably, at least I had grown as a writer.

METAMORPHOSIS

As a creature of developed habits who acknowledged daily that I wanted to transform every area of my life, I was afraid of change and what might happen if I stepped outside my comfort zone. Uncertain whether my busy mind could handle anything other than what it was used to, I was also afraid of what would happen if things *didn't* change.

I felt stuck and exhausted, living each day without the appreciation it deserved. I was tuckered out, living under the requirements of my anxious thoughts, stubborn personality, and the inability to maintain the thing I desired most in life: peace of mind.

My family of four—my almost-teen son, my one-year-old daughter, my boyfriend, and I—shared a 934-square-foot townhouse, and I could feel the walls closing in around me. I was still attending school online while I stayed at home with the baby, and without a second income, I was hesitant to move. I had rented the unit for about eleven years, and staying in the cramped, confining box was more comfortable than the prospect of a mortgage we might not be prepared to pay.

Faced with a crowded reality, I wondered if we would ever have a place of our own. I felt the need for more than just a spacious new home. A part of me was empty, constantly living in the past and suffering from what had come from it. I was miserable inside, and many days I couldn't even get out of my own way if something triggered me.

Since I never knew what would cause a disruption in my day, every morning, noon, and night differed from the last. I was always slightly on edge, waiting to be punished for some old transgression.

Filled with memories of the past, I was a prisoner of my circumstances, never able to see a way free of constant fear. I couldn't see a light guiding me out of the darkness that engulfed me.

I felt captive of the web I had spun, as though the good parts of my life were slipping out of my reach more each day. The six-headed dragon I had birthed from the duo of traumatic events followed me everywhere. Steadily breathing havoc down my neck. Shooting its flamed breath at me every time I attempted to escape to a pleasant thought, the idea of successfully fleeing seemed impossible. The years of therapy I had sought to help with my overwhelming thoughts were no match for its fiery hold.

Countless hours spent on a perfectly positioned loveseat overlooking the scenic Maine woods failed to provide the safety net I needed to catch me. Often, the more I tried listening to the advice of medical professionals, the further I fell. I couldn't wrap my head around Cognitive Behavioral Therapy. It just wasn't for me.

Even though I desperately wanted to change, I left my appointments feeling worse than when I entered their chambers of strategic mind training. Not that they weren't knowledgeable or didn't have the best of intentions, but I needed something different, something to wake me up from the deadly sleep it had mired me in for so long. I needed a positive push to launch me into a better understanding of life and what I could become *if* I actually tried and focused.

Every day, I would pretend to be happy and free from the thoughts that "used" to bind me, but it was a lie. They still wrapped me up in a blanket of terror, trapped by anxiety that smothered me like a straitjacket. Inside, my soul was screaming for something more. Inside, I was screaming to be saved.

As my toes hung off the edge of the step, waiting to hit the hardwood floor beneath them, something inside of me shifted. I sensed a firmness of confidence growing within, spreading over my insecurities like ivy on a brick wall.

In order to discover a piece of me I knew was missing, I decided it was time to make time to read and embrace the opportunity of a new way of living. Dirty diapers, grocery shopping, schooling, housework, fear of change, and learning to manage the growing sarcasm of my eleven-year-old would always be there, regardless of how I allocated my time. It was time to focus on myself and who I wanted to be.

With optimism paving the way for my eager eyes, I opened the hard cover that bound the mysterious teachings together and turned the stiff pages. As I felt the roughness of the paper fibers smear against my fingers, I could already sense the magic vibrating between them.

The excitement danced off my fingertips as I turned to the first chapter. I remembered when I first heard about the book a decade earlier. A couple of my closest friends back then couldn't stop raving about how *The Secret* had transformed their lives, and how all their wildest dreams were coming true after they learned to manifest them.

I sat on the edge of their lumpy futon in a living room cozy for two, lost in the intricate pattern of the tapestry hanging in front of the open window. Leaning forward to light a candle, they explained how they had manifested their black BMW in no time at all. They strove to get their fascinating findings across to me in a way that made sense, to make me understand that the Law of Attraction was real and that all I needed to know to get started sat patiently between the pages in black and white.

Although I was intrigued by the basic concept of what they were trying to teach, it wasn't enough to peel me away from my entanglements. Back then, I was young and thought I knew all I needed to know about life. Since I tuned out anyone seeking to sway me in one direction or another, I wasn't ready to hear what was being presented to me that day. I was too consumed in my world, stubbornly resisting the idea that someone else might know a tool or trick that could help *me* better *my* life.

Always focused on what wasn't rather than what was and what could be, I was content knowing that I would most likely be stuck in a small town for the rest of my life. The possibility of attending and graduating from college seemed slim, which left me facing a future that consisted of waiting on tables, depending on the kindness of others to make or break my bank account that day.

Having shoved their offerings of a "real" revelation aside that afternoon, I spent the next several years living in emotional, physical, and financial inconsistency. I never gave what they tried to share a second thought until my dear friend brought it up weeks before my thirty-fourth birthday.

After I had complained about all the things that had gone wrong in adulthood, how everything still wasn't what I wanted it to be, she offered a piece of advice that would lead to self-achievement, well-being, and prosperity.

Though I was quick to attack any suggestions that alluded to the abundance of prosperity she promised from the teachings, she said if I was "ready," she had a book for me to read called *The Secret*. She informed me it had to do with manifestation and suggested I read it when I could, no pressure, and let her know what I thought when I was done.

I stood on the edge of the bottom step that humid July morning, feeling as if I were a hamster on an endless wheel of worries, and finally let go of my frustration. Like a force of gravity yanking heavy matter toward its core, something inside of me lit up as I heard the book speaking to me, urging me to pick it up. An inner voice told me it was time, and I was ready to hear what it said. I allowed the emotions of intimidation blow past me like smoke and, in a fraction of a second, I easily pushed aside the idea of not having any time. Suddenly I had all the time in the world! I was dedicated to claiming the knowledge of what the book offered.

As I marveled at the fact I had changed a part of me so easily, with no feelings of doubt, I felt a small wave of clarity come over me. In that moment, as I let the awareness rain down upon me, I was excited about life for the first time in years! In the tiny living room I shared with my family, a newness was blossoming.

I ran over to the couch and plopped down enthusiastically. Spread out comfortably with a giant mug of coffee by my side, I took a deep breath and read a book published back in 2006 by an author named Rhonda Byrne.

It suggested a unique way of living saturated with abundance in all avenues: happiness, love, wealth, health, and achieving dreams that often seemed out of reach, and I was sold after the first chapter. I quickly peeled back page after page, nearly cutting my fingers on the sharp paper edges of enthusiasm and absorbed everything I was reading like a sponge soaking up spilled milk.

The Law of Attraction was a natural law of the Universe that was always moving. As vibrational beings full of energy, we dictated our own frequencies that were then sent out into the Universe. The thoughts circling our mind and the emotions that filled us determined our vibrational level. Based upon how we felt and what we thought, we would attract other "like" things on that same vibrational frequency.

Positive thoughts and feelings would bring about a high level of vibration, blessing us with similar things and events. Negative thoughts and feelings would bring low-level vibrations, attracting dull and inconvenient circumstances. Simply put, we were exactly what we thought about. Researching further on my own, I learned this phenomenon was offered to everyone regardless of race, age, gender, and religious belief, and that it provided unimaginable ways to bring more of what we focused on in our lives through the thoughts we created. Through the power of thought, the Law of Attraction would always deliver more "like" things.

I was drawn to the idea that this universal law existed, and I had a driving curiosity about what led Rhonda to write a book about it in the first place, so I did some digging. After suffering a series of traumatic events in 2004, she had received a book from her daughter called *The Science of Getting Rich* by Wallace D.

Wattles. When she discovered a secret explaining the laws of the Universe, she was intrigued and felt compelled to learn more about the principles of attraction.

She researched back thousands of years and found that religious believers ascribing to Christianity, Buddhism, Judaism and more, as well as ancient Egyptians and Babylonians, had left written teachings about the magnetizing law's existence. One was the Emerald Tablet, a stone dating back to 3000 BC that spoke of the mysterious law that most who knew kept hidden for themselves but was available for others to discover.

As she put the law into practice, she saw changes in her life take place for the better almost instantly and realized it was her purpose to share the universal secret and its principles with the world. She collaborated with others who knew of the secret and, combining their collected scientific laws, knowledge of metaphysics, and personal experiences, Rhonda and her team of reputable teachers concocted an inspirational read. Produced in over fifty languages and with a staggering thirty-four million copies in print, she took the world by storm with her teachings. *The Secret* stayed on the *New York Times* bestsellers list for over two hundred weeks after its initial release. The accomplishments and passion of this one woman fascinated me. Her research was not only impressive, but legitimate, and I marveled at what she had created and couldn't wait to read more.

She had dug deep with her findings, sharing quotes from a wide range of sources who showed they too believed in the power to think something into existence. Albert Einstein felt that "Imagination is everything. It is the preview of life's coming attractions." The Buddha said, "All that we are is a result of what we have thought."

As I read her chosen quotes repeatedly, I tried to remember a time when I had believed something positive about myself, my life, and what I had contributed to the world. All I could think of was my children. But if Einstein and the Buddha were right, it was no wonder that the "coming attractions" I had experienced were anything but likable, and my life currently matched my beliefs that nothing would ever work out well for me.

The wheels were turning on the concept that I was living through the thoughts and feelings that consumed me most. With each page, I was falling more in love, especially when a small section of the book metaphorically compared the laws of the Universe to the story of Aladdin and his magical lamp. I had been obsessed with the familiar story as a child and still had my Aladdin coffee mug purchased at Disney back in the nineties. I remembered wishing and dreaming of all the things I had wanted, imagining a world where all I had to do was rub a miniature gold lamp and out would come the genie, ready to grant all my desires. As explained by Rhonda and contributor James Ray, the genie who granted all of Aladdin's wishes was simply the Law of Attraction, bringing forth all the things we thought about most. Regardless of whether it was positive or negative, whatever we predominantly thought, spoke, and acted upon, the genie/Universe would deliver in likeness, every time, and without question.

Still warm with the pleasant childhood memory dancing about in my mind, I wondered if the genie was indeed the Universe granting all that was desired and undesired through thought, how one would go about doing so? How would one exactly think their wishes into existence?

With an answer for every question of the diligent reader, broken down into an easy, three-step process, the best-selling author explained just how simple it was to manifest things you desired. First, in order to launch a manifestation out into the Universe, you must be clear about what was desired and *ask* for it.

Being clear and concise about what was being asked was key because, if wants and desires were indecisive, a mixed signal would be sent out to the Universe, altering what you were trying to attract. And you didn't have to ask repeatedly for something.

Like placing an order at a favorite eatery, you only had to order once, expecting the meal to be cooked and knowing that it would.

Believing was the next step required in manifesting your desires. Believing was important because it showed that, no matter what was going on in your life or what you lacked, you had faith and trusted that desires would come into reality when they were supposed to. Believing was not worrying how or when manifestations would appear but understanding that no desire was too big or too small for the Universe to deliver. That it would come because you asked. Believing was about acting as if you had already received it.

Receiving was the last step to releasing desires. Acting as if you had already received would bring feelings of joy, excitement, gratitude, and the bliss you would feel when it arrived. Experiencing the feelings before it appeared would attract the "feel good" vibration with which your desires resonated, ultimately lining you up to sync with other like vibrations.

Believing that you had received meant to feel it with every cell of your being. Almost every contributor voiced the same notion: it was essential to feel as if you had already received what you desired.

Rhonda included well-known excerpts from the Bible: Matthew 21:22, "Whatsoever ye shall ask in prayer, believing, ye shall receive," and Mark 11:24, "What things soever ye desire, when ye pray, believe that ye receive them, and ye shall have them."

A spot-on reference to her three-step theory, both excerpts affirmed that if a desire was asked and prayed for, believing the desire would be received and feeling as if it had, it would eventually be brought forth into reality.

Raised Catholic, I recognized the Bible verses, and for the first time, I understood the meaning behind them and how they connected to the universal magnetic force of attraction. That whatever I wanted in life, I would receive, if I believed I would.

It was interesting that apostles Matthew and Mark had taken the time to document something so few knew about back then . . . "the secret." I thought of all the parishioners from the congregation I belonged to as a child and wondered if they had ever fully understood the verses and their profound meaning!

It was even more interesting that the new interpretation of the verses didn't seem to focus on religion, but promoted the idea that there was a common denominator between people from the past and present believing in a higher, unseen power. The Bible verses and the Emerald Tablet were about those looking to leave their stories behind for the world to see, acknowledge, and better understand the higher power that existed.

With the basic understanding of how far the fascinating law traced back and how it brought forth whatever one believed and thought most about—fear, worry, doubt, happiness, love, wealth, health, joy—I recalled moments when I had unknowingly set it in motion.

I could see times in my life where things had gone smoothly, one great thing after another. Then, there were other moments where everything had gone wrong. According to the book, one could tell how they were using the magical law, productively or unproductively, by examining how they felt. And for the last several years, I had been using the law consistently to my disadvantage.

I felt sick at the fact that my own creative thoughts and instilled beliefs had most likely been blocking me from living the life I desired to have; that my patterns of dreading the things I *didn't* want to happen in life had only brought them closer to me through negative attraction. For years, I had inadvertently been paving the path to my future with my own fearful thoughts. I was living in a tornado of negativity, sucking me in and spitting me out every chance it got.

With my mind spinning, it was easy for me to see why I had been living in such a slump for what had seemed like forever. As I read the engrossing text, I understood that everything I had been living I had simply and easily attracted on my own, both good and bad.

As I sat on the couch, rocking my body into a calmer state, I understood why my relationship was stuck after hitting the two-year mark. I understood why I wasn't a published author. I understood why I was so moody all the time, picking fights whenever I had a chance to prove someone "wrong" to make myself look knowledgeable. I finally understood why, no matter how hard I tried to remove myself from the pile of dirt and debris I had swept myself into over the years, I could never seem to get out of it. I didn't recognize the connection between vibrational energy, humans, feelings, thoughts, and universal law until reading Byrne's perfectly written account of it.

Holding a high vibration was the key to successfully attracting the good I desired in life. But I had been wearing a honey suit, attracting all things grizzly in the woods of my existence. With my constant negativity, persistently avoiding all positive thinking, concentrating on all the things I didn't want, I had created the perfect momentum to collect buckets of manure.

The Law of Attraction worked in both directions of thought process—good and bad—and the riveting self-help book couldn't stress it enough. The law never stopped working and didn't understand what you "didn't" want. It only understood what you thought of most, which was why you had to be careful with the words you spoke in addition to the thoughts you held captive in your mind.

The more you thought and spoke of what you "didn't" want, the more things you were trying to avoid would appear, and I had done just that. Every complaint, worry, doubt, argument, and lack of belief that things could never change for the better had painted a picture that was dark and depressing—and I was living in it.

Dr. Fred Alan Wolf, award-winning author and quantum physicist, explained in *The Secret* his understanding that our thoughts create images in our mind. Those thoughts are then reflected as our life experiences, which meant that I was my worst enemy, preventing the dreams I desired from reaching me. Not my traumas or past life experiences, but me.

Looking over the basic examples given by Dr. Wolf, I could see clearly that the more I complained about what I didn't want, like debt, sickness, and exhaustion, the more debt, sickness, and exhaustion I would draw to myself. He suggested a simple adjustment in word choices was a great place to command change and that individuals could do so by using "I am" statements.

Wolf's "I am" statement consisted of following the phrase with something positive like telling oneself: "I am healthy, I am well, I am full of abundance." Wolf claimed that the "I am" approach would be constructive wording versus destructive that humans often use.

Rhonda also stressed that wording was very important. Saying things that reflected negation like "I don't want. . . ." or "I can't handle. . . ." would only draw more of those things, because the Universe didn't understand negation. What the Universe recognized were the predominant thoughts and feelings you projected.

I took a few moments to digest everything I had brought upon myself in recent months. I recalled every negative thought that had produced an unruly feeling, creating a crapshoot in the universal game of attraction that I had been unaware I was playing in.

The invisible light bulb hanging over my head lit up faster than a ring of fire. All I had to do was change my thoughts, *now*. Whatever I was thinking *now* in the present moment would either lift me high to the vibration of my desired beliefs or sink me deep beneath the ocean floor. What I needed to do was rip off the rearview mirror that followed me everywhere I went and tempted me to look back on the things that terrified me most.

Reliving traumatic events time and time again had altered my state of mind, convincing my consciousness that bad things would keep happening to me. That car crashes and death would always be the norm. If I changed my beliefs, I could change my thoughts and ultimately change my feelings, leading to a new, favorable, vibrational level; a vibrational level that granted the peace of mind to enjoy every moment of time instead of fearing it.

I knew it would be a challenge to change the negative thought process I had developed over the years to a place of consistent positivity. But just like making the time to read, I knew that if I really wanted to transform my belief system, I could.

It seemed logical that slow and steady would ultimately win the war of intrusive thoughts, but I found old patterns crept in just as I was getting my footing, whispering in my ear that my clock was ticking. When I found myself overwhelmed with anxiety, Lisa Nichols's words in *The Secret* brought comfort and ease to my churning mind. According to Lisa, beloved motivational speaker and best-selling author, time was on our side, and the terrifying ideas of all the what ifs could be overcome immediately with beautiful thoughts and feelings of what I wanted in my life *today*.

In order to refocus my mind, I let the feeling of doomed time slip away from the accumulated years of misery I had experienced and put my attention back on how incorporating the mystical law into my life would change everything for the better, *now*. Accepting that both feelings and thoughts were the roots that held us in the soil that tethered us, I was ready to see the miraculous changes happen in my life that everyone spoke of in the book I couldn't put down.

Sharing amazing stories of established individuals and their rise to success through ultimate manifestation, the television producer's book also included heartwarming stories of miracles, like the story of Morris Goodman, a man who had all odds against him.

In March of 1981, Morris Goodman crashed the plane he was flying and survived. Left with his spinal cord crushed, and both his first and second vertebrae broken, he was paralyzed, unable even to drink or eat.

His diaphragm was damaged so severely that Goodman couldn't even breath on his own, which resulted in him being ventilated. He could only blink his eyes, and the physicians referred to him as a "vegetable" and told Goodman that he would be that way for the rest of his life.

Unsatisfied with the description of life he was given by doctors, Goodman refused to believe his diagnosis and decided that he would create his own prognosis. He envisioned himself not as a lifeless being lying still in a hospital bed, but he began to see himself just as he had been before his accident. He held onto the vision of himself walking out of the hospital and living a normal life.

Aware that his mind was the only thing functioning smoothly, he realized that his thoughts would be the first piece in his healing puzzle. Telling himself to breathe deeply, rejecting the idea that his diaphragm no longer worked on its own, in a matter of time Goodman was taken off his ventilator after showing he could breathe on his own.

Doctors were speechless and had no words of explanation for the medical miracle. Goodman continued to focus on his goal, which was to walk out of the hospital unassisted by Christmas. When Christmas came, he followed through with his set goal. Walking out of the hospital on his own, Goodman proved that will and determination of the human mind was perhaps the most powerful tool of all.

Quoted as saying, "Man becomes what he thinks about," Morris Goodman's story not only showed that it was miraculous, but that perseverance over anything in life would conquer what tried to defeat you.

As I thought about my past and how it had led me down a comfortable path of playing the victim, I realized how I blamed my patterns of anxiety on the tragic accident that had taken my boyfriend's life and what happened after the dust had settled. Instead of seeing that I could live a life of freedom, walking around without the past clinging to me like a leech, I saw a giant white flag surrendering to the idea that I would never be happy or have the things I preferred. I had given up a long time ago and easily.

When confronted by family or therapists with ways to help "ease" the functioning of my mind, I blamed the awful traumas for creating the new characteristics of my personality. I used them as an excuse as to why I could never change. The "daily dreads" had become part of me, controlling everything I did, and I had let them do so with no fight at all.

Learning of Goodman's inspiring story did something to me. I saw how I was using the variety of traumas as a reason to continue living in a fog. I saw how I refused to create any light to shine through, showing a way to happiness, because it was easier to fall back on the patterns I created.

As I flashed back to all the times I played victim to my circumstances, I now understood the potential I'd had all long to help heal on my own. I carried the ability to heal from the inside out by using the strength and power of thought to better my existence.

It was fascinating to wrap my head around the new idea of self-help that I had discovered. The stories I was reading about self-healing took me to a whole other level of believing, and it felt good. It felt even better when contributor Bob Proctor mentioned that disease couldn't live in a body that was emotionally healthy, and that was important for me to understand. He pointed out the word "disease" simply meant that the body was not "in-ease" but out of it, and that the word told us so just by how it was spelt, "dis-ease."

If I altered my thought perception drastically, I realized my body would become healthier. I had health, but what I wanted most was the peace of mind that would come by dissolving my dis-eased thoughts and knowing that I *had* health because I accepted nothing but.

I wanted my mind restored, and by doing so, I would help my body in the process. It would take constant practice to shift the thousands of thoughts that poured out of me like an unleashed Hoover Dam, but if I worked at it, I knew I could do it. It seemed incomprehensible to think that the mind could create so many thoughts. However, according to *The Secret* contributor Marci Shimoff, researchers found that sixty thousand thoughts were detected to enter the human mind daily.

As I tried to visualize this, all I could think of was that I was a tree with beautiful limbs, and the buds that I sprouted represented the thoughts I was thinking. The thoughts would blossom regardless of whether they were thoughts that served me or ones that didn't.

Either way, once sprouted, a leaf would grow from it, and if I correctly nourished the buds with the right amount of water and sunlight, the leaves would gloriously grow into earthy shades of beautiful green, filling the tree abundantly. If the blooming tree lacked what it needed to prosper, it would stand sparse and alone, which was exactly what my life would be if I didn't get my shit together and change my habitual thoughts.

The fear of deteriorating health was driving me crazy. If I could weed out the health anxieties and fill them with confident images of wellness instead, and do so by carefully choosing the motives in my mind, I'd finally be free, free to think of what I craved instead of what I didn't.

In that moment, picturing the leaves on my boughs growing tall and wide, I could feel my emotions shift to a different vibrational level. All it took was one thought and the notion that I could change anything and everything in my life *if* I wanted to.

What Rhonda's tell-all promised was that as long as you didn't let your everyday surroundings—including people and circumstances—alter your vibration, you would see magnificent changes come into your life bringing about love, good fortune, health, and more. If you stayed on the path of positivity and altered your response to unwanted things around you, the Universe would move people, places, and circumstances to your advantage.

Thoroughly described in the book, our minds were magnets pulling the things we thought about right into our existence, which was why the concept of the Law of Attraction was so enticing! If focused and aware, anyone could create anything they ever wanted, and it was easy to do. Through controlled thought, I too could create a better way of life.

It was important to understand that anything was possible and equally important that feelings of *gratitude* were necessary. Mentioned several times in Byrne's book, gratitude was a core component of using the universal law because it led to the path of receiving more things to be grateful about.

Rhonda quoted author Wallace Wattles as having said, "The daily practice of gratitude is one of the conduits by which your wealth will come to you."

Reading Wattles's quote struck a nerve in me. I realized how grateful I was when I looked around. I had food, clothes, water, health, love, money, and material items that I enjoyed. I had everything to be grateful for, which meant that I should have been beaming rays of gratitude from head to toe for the last several years of my life, but I hadn't. I was too busy pushing away the things I didn't want, unknowingly ignoring all that I already had.

In that moment of understanding that I was indeed already abundant, and in many aspects of my life, I was appreciative for the times I had taken my abundance for granted, because it taught me to never turn a blind eye again. I told myself that I would always see and appreciate the abundance I had. I would say "thank you" frequently, showing signs of gratitude for things both big and small, right down to the overflowing silverware drawer that snagged every time I opened it.

I would stop complaining about the things I didn't have, like a bigger house and more money. Instead, I would know that I could bring more of both into my life by being thankful for the space I was in and the money already sitting in my bank account, whether it be one dollar or a thousand.

If I wanted more of something, like money, I understood that fretting about the amount I didn't have only brought more financial things to fret about. Trusting and relying on the Universe to provide and inspire me with ways to earn money was the ticket to financial freedom.

Another contributor, David Schirmer, a wealth specialist, said he constantly envisioned checks coming to him in the mail. An odd strategy at first glance, it made sense because visualizing was a part of creating something that wasn't yet true. Before Schirmer knew it, he had checks coming to him in the mail just as he had imagined. He had brought reality to his desires because of where he had held his thoughts. Carefully creating, he matched the vibration of what he wanted, summoning other "like" things into his life.

Intrigued by Schirmer's playful money tip, I made use of the spam credit card offers that always flooded my mailbox and taped a fake check for forty thousand dollars to my fridge. Looking at the check daily, I knew checks like that could be mine if I believed I deserved them and trusted they would come. I needed to encompass feelings of gratitude despite what I didn't have.

Besides his check visualization strategy, Schirmer also shared his experience of how he would always attract the perfect parking spot. Ninety-five percent of the time, he would just pull right in; the other 5 percent, he had to wait a few minutes. Through visualization and expecting to receive what he was thinking, he had placed himself in alignment with his desires and manifested the very thing he wanted: a killer parking spot.

Delighted with what I was learning, it inspired me to change everything in my world. Suddenly, a new person was being born inside me. I felt moved to donate more items to charity than I normally did because I finally saw how much I had to give. I was excited to finish college, despite having taken years and years to do it. Most importantly, I was thrilled at the fact that I could take the knowledge I had learned and incorporate it into my home life. I felt like I was on the right path.

My mouth fell open when I came across the section about *inspiration*. Bob Doyle, multimedia creator producing programs on the Law of Attraction, affirmed that occasionally, *action* may be called to you through *inspiration*. Doyle said that sometimes you could wake on a new day and find your manifestations waiting for you. Other times, you might feel inspired to take *action*.

Adding to Doyle's statement, Rhonda wrote that *inspired action* didn't mean to force the receiving rather than trust that the Universe would provide it. It meant to trust the impulses coming from within. It meant to flow with the river, to effortlessly take steps toward one's goal when moved to do so versus swimming against the current trying to *make* things happen. Inspired action was about trusting gut feelings and doing so with ease. It was also about not giving up and pushing forward, just like Jack Canfield had done.

Jack Canfield's journey was a true success story with his writing and using the captivating law to achieve ultimate success with publication. Selling over 110 million copies in the US and Canada and over 500 million worldwide to date, Canfield's book series has brought happiness to millions. Literally.

When I was growing up, *Chicken Soup for the Soul* was in every window I walked past at the local plaza. Giant cutout cardboards hanging in bookstores stood tall, luring dedicated readers in, scampering to pick up their copy. On his YouTube channel, Canfield told of all the times they rejected his idea for the soulful book series, but that he didn't let that keep him down.

"Reject rejection" he said proudly in *The Secret* film, which was something I hadn't done during the first round of querying agents to represent my manuscript. Instead, I had pushed it aside and let it sit for four years without revisiting it.

As it opened up doors to mentors and stories I never knew existed, *The Secret* motivated a part of me that had been forgotten for some time. The explanation of *inspired action* paired with the story of Jack Canfield generated the intention of picking up the book I had minimally tried and failed to publish. I related to Canfield because I wanted to do what he had achieved, write an amazing book, help millions of people, and enjoy financial freedom.

I wanted to succeed so I could help other people, not just my family. I wanted to do other things like create a school charity. After working at a public school and seeing how many children went without clean clothes, fresh haircuts, and enough food, I had dreamed about one day helping.

I could see myself succeeding, just as Canfield had. I could see my dreams of becoming a published author and philanthropist coming true if *I took the action* to do so.

Just as he had placed the title of his book in plain sight with written suggestions that it was already a best seller, I did the same. I wrote the name of my manuscript on a piece of paper, grabbed a Stephen King book, and made my book jacket. Then I positioned the homemade cover just below the #1 bestseller label, secured it with an elastic band, and set it on my kitchen counter so I could look at and feel it every chance I walked by. I knew *feeling* it would engender happiness, as if publication were already mine.

I decided it was time to practice and begin the new life I realized I was destined to live, one filled with bliss, success, and peace of mind. It was time to get moving, and I knew just how to get the ball rolling. I took what I had learned over the last three days—*asking, believing, receiving, gratitude,* and *inspired action*—and decided to first apply it using David Schirmer's parking space story. A parking spot seemed simple enough to attract, so I put it to the test, hoping to defeat the slight doubts I had about how quickly the miracle law could work.

Knowing that I would make a trip to the grocery store soon, I created my attraction ahead of time, just as Schirmer had suggested. In addition to *asking* and *believing* that I had already *received* the prime parking spot, I felt the feeling of pulling into a close parking space made only for me. I visualized a sign with my name on it planted firmly in the concrete. I felt the excitement of hearing my tires come to rest on the dusty pavement so close to the store. I felt the discarded pieces of wood chips from the landscaping tap the sides of my ankles as the wind blew them about. I felt the appreciation of only having to push the baby stroller just a little way.

A few days later, when the trip to the store arrived, I was looking forward to what I normally considered a dreaded family chore instead of cursing it. I was ready to claim my spot. On the short drive over to Hannaford, I kept envisioning the spot as mine. There were a few moments of doubt but, for most of the three-minute drive, I remained confident.

As I pulled up to the traffic light while signaling my left turn, my stomach fluttered with butterflies, eager to see if the spot I had thought of was indeed waiting for me. The light, which ordinarily took forever, turned green almost immediately, and I chuckled that my positive thinking had already started a path of ease for my shopping trip.

With Van Halen cranking from the speakers of my Jeep, I veered into the giant lot packed with cars and headed toward the store. Banishing the immediate hesitation that my space was taken, I rapidly replaced it with the affirmation, "There is a spot for me." I crept through the narrow lot, my fingers gripping the leather steering wheel as I closed in on my intended space. Taking a deep breath, I inched forward and saw the minivan that had stolen my manifestation.

I threw the Jeep in reverse and made my way back to a spot I had seen but tried to ignore when I passed it. I got out of the car, longing for the feeling of chipped wood playing tag with the wind, tickling my ankles and sandaled feet, and I solemnly extracted the car seat. With the carrier in the crevice of my arm, I awkwardly began the journey toward the front of the store. Waddling, bouncing the baby carrier off my hip with every step I took, I wondered which part of the self-sabotage had unmanifested my perfect parking place. Turning around to look at my white Jeep sitting in the alternative spot I had thought of, just in case my initial spot occupied, I struggled to identify a reason for what had transpired.

Clearly, it wasn't a coincidence I had received my second choice, and a wave of awareness came over me. I remembered the contributors stressed just how abundant the Universe was, and that there was enough to go around for everyone. The occupant of the van had not been a thief, but somehow a test.

The universal force of attraction had worked just fine. It hadn't failed me, but my trust in *receiving* had. I had manifested just fine, but then doubted what would be available. *I alone* was responsible for what had happened. Even though I mostly thought productively, there was still a slight part of me that said I wouldn't get the spot. That the first time attracting wouldn't be as easy as everyone said. I had expected to get my second choice, parking farther back from the spot I had wanted, and that was exactly what I got.

Chuckling at the irony that my small doubt had delivered my Plan B, I approached the spot I had initially chosen and immediately stopped in my tracks as I watched the taillights on the silver minivan light up. All I could think was, *Son of a b—*! Within seconds, the van began to slowly back out of the spot with a kind smile and a simple wave from the driver. If only I had waited and circled the lot, the spot would have been available for me, and I wouldn't be walking, struggling to carry the weight of my hefty one-year-old halfway across the football field-sized lot.

As I watched the van disappear, I smiled, thankful for what had just happened. Standing with the scorching sun shining down and sweat droplets the size of fresh-water pearls beading down my face, I promised myself that from that day forward, I would fully commit and trust in the things that I wanted to attract. I would make certain my mind was clear of any clouds of doubt, and know that in time, when it was supposed to happen, the Universe would bear all the fruit I desired. Even something as small as a parking place.

I spent the next six weeks practicing what I had learned, remembering to take my personal experience with me. I could feel a change already, but most intriguing was the idea that in a year's time I could be exactly where I desired to be.

I was ready to up the ante and go from attracting parking spaces to attracting literary agents. Gathering the courage to take the inspired action from Jack Canfield's story, I forged ahead with my dream of becoming an author. I reworked my entire manuscript, giving it a complete makeover in less than six weeks. I clipped, gutted, scrapped, and rewrote the sixty-thousand-word memoir I had lost faith in and turned it into the shorter, more emotional story that it should have been. I described my traumas and spoke honestly of how deeply they had affected me. I spoke of the devastation I had felt when Damin died, and how my life had fallen apart. I made the book more intimate so others with similar experiences would know they weren't alone and that everyone, at some point, goes through dark periods.

Then I asked a family friend who is a published author to look at my manuscript and offer her honest opinion. After finishing the book in one sitting, she emailed the next day to tell me how much she loved it and that she was proud of me. Stating she saw many books in me, she suggested I try my hand at penning romance novels, as my steamy love scenes had really caught her attention.

She encouraged me to create fictional characters and storylines, spinning my tales of passion from there. She also suggested giving short stories a try, as she had fallen in love with some of the real-life characters in the book.

She said that I would find a publisher, and it was just a matter of finding the right one. She advised me that writing was my gift and to let no one tell me otherwise. This was the confirmation I needed to actively pursue my ambition. It was what I needed to hear . . . that my writing spoke to others the same way it did to me. My mother always told me that my work was great, but that was different because she was my mom and was always supportive of my dreams.

I had also met two writing professors while attending college. One was a friend and mentor who graciously helped me with an earlier book and who had a way of bringing out the best in me as a writer. The other professor shared with me on the last day of her class that she was certain she would see my books in stores one day.

Even though I had constant support throughout the stages of my writing development, for some reason, when my family friend shared her feelings about the rewritten manuscript, a strong solid wave of assurance swept over me because a published author thought I had what it took to be recognized in the literary world.

With an army of purpose and confidence behind me, I was ready to submit the newly revised manuscript. I scoured the Internet, researching the best agencies for my genre and viewing the profile of every agent who sounded promising. As I scrolled through the digital diaries of the agent's likes, dislikes, educational achievements, and job history, I discovered there was more to querying a book than just typing up a brief bio and hitting send on an attachment. Every agent wanted something different!

Working constantly on my query letter, hook line, synopsis, and proposal, I spent the last weeks of summer editing, cutting, and pasting until I thought everything was perfect. Over the course of the next three weeks, I sent out over a hundred queries, believing that my hard work would pay off and launch a fresh career and a fresh beginning for my family. After all, I had done my homework and then some, so my chances of landing at least one book deal within the large group I had petitioned seemed high.

I called to tell my dear friend that the new manuscript had been signed, sealed, and delivered to the Universe; all that remained was to wait for the flood of responses I would receive back. She told me how proud of me she was for taking the giant step to rewrite the book, and how much she thought I had changed in such a short amount of time. In addition, she said she was sending me a new book to read.

Similar in scope to the gripping book that had entranced me by using the power of thought for attraction, this focused more on healing life's traumas and understanding how the body connected to the things we internally held on to. She explained it was one of her favorite books, one you didn't have to read from cover to cover. You could close your eyes and randomly pick a page, trusting that the Universe had led you to what you needed to read that day.

Finally, she reminded me to think as if I had already received the request for representation; not that I was ready to receive, but that I already had.

Four days later, a large manila envelope with an Amazon logo greeted me. I ran along the pathway back to the condo, tearing open the package, eager to get my hands on my friend's favorite book. My eyes lit up when I saw the vibrant colors of the front cover. There were giant hearts filled with delightful messages, beautiful gold lettering, and a peaceful bird fluttering in the right corner. It was everything I'd imagined it would be and more!

Stepping inside and slamming the door shut, I plopped down on the overstuffed chair my brother had bought me for my thirty-third birthday and began leafing through the pages. Remembering what my dear friend had said, I opened the book at random and let the Universe decide where I would start.

As I skimmed through the colorful illustrations, I could see why the book was a favorite of hers. Not only were the illustrations different on every page, but every single color of the rainbow had been generously and randomly spread throughout. Every page sang a different song, which made the book exciting, bright, and full of life, which was just what I needed. Louise Hay's *You Can Heal Your Life* was going to do just that . . . heal my life!

With magical drawings of animals, people, flowers, and more, Louise had outdone herself. I felt like I was reading a children's book for grown-ups. The watercolor-style pictures painted a soft trance as I roughly glanced at the pages.

Broken into five sections, the book covered everything about relationships, health, work, and finances, and in the final section, decoded the root of every possible physical ailment. It was an encyclopedia, dictionary, and spiritual guide all wrapped up in one. In its section dedicated to dis-ease, the book had an answer for everything from nail-biting to hemorrhoids to insomnia, and an affirmation to wipe it clean from the body.

I closed the book and held it tight to my chest, knowing in my heart it was exactly what I needed for my next step toward spiritual growth. *The Secret* had awakened my mind, and now it was time to allow this spiritual pioneer into my life, letting her work her magic just as she had for millions of others.

I opened my laptop and searched for her website to learn more about the leading lady of wellness. Louise Hay was a pioneer in the world of self-help books. In fact, her *New York Times* bestseller, *You Can Heal Your Life*, written in 1984, had sold over forty million copies by 2012. Clearly, the message it carried was strong and meaningful. Overcoming obstacles in her life, she was confident when it came time to apply her beliefs, but more importantly, she was confident that her ways would help others.

Jack Canfield had said that helping others was primary in the expansion of an individual's wealth through the Law of Attraction. In addition to helping readers of her own books, Louise Hay also created a foundation to help those suffering from AIDS. Warm with happiness, I closed my Google search tab, picked up the book, and continued reading the bestseller.

Louise began at the foundation, explaining that our childhood had a tremendous impact on who we were as adults. Stressing that "we are all victims of victims," she explained that if our parents didn't know how to love themselves, it would be impossible for them to teach us how to love ourselves. Without that, there will always be the feeling of "not being good enough" to enjoy life the way we deserved to.

Taking a moment to reflect on my childhood, I realized I had lots of splendid memories interspersed with a few unpleasant ones. My household was always filled with love and support, and I had everything a child could want or need. My parents divorced before I was born, and I lived with my mother in central Maine, with my father a couple of hours away in Portland. I saw him here and there, but it was mostly her beliefs that built my idea of what the world was about.

I was taught to be honest and kind to others, to follow the rules, and to appreciate the things I had—in other words, Parenting 101. My mom and I had a great relationship, straying from our closeness during my later teenage years when I needed space or felt I had to discover things on my own, but mostly, we shared a healthy mother–daughter bond.

My mother was a literacy technician, teaching reading and writing at the local public school, so she could work the same schedule as my school hours. In doing so, she turned down better-paying jobs and left her own licensed nursery school to ensure that she was always around for me. We enjoyed shopping together, painting our nails, doing one another's hair, and indulging in weekend home spas. With mud masks covering our faces, we gorged on homemade popcorn. We had fun together no matter what we did, and my friends always loved coming over to share in our laughter.

As for my father, he did the best he could to make up for lost time, which often meant showering me with gifts. His absence was the driving force behind the expensive makeup, the Tommy Hilfiger hoodies, and the freedom to sip a beer with him now and then in my teen years. Sometimes, time spent with my dad was shared with his son by his second wife, a little over two years younger than me. Because we didn't see each other as often as we liked, we played up the sibling rivalry as best we could when I traveled down to Portland for a visit, and I enjoyed his presence no matter how much we teased and taunted one another.

My dad worked various jobs before landing a solid one at Idexx, an international company that specialized in veterinary medicine, and he stayed employed there for twenty-one years. The inconsistency of his job history paralleled our relationship until his parenting patterns changed for the better and my birthday cards started coming on time. But it wasn't until I was in my late twenties that our relationship really blossomed, and I learned more about him as a man and a father. I had come to understand and forgive him for his absences, which had helped to shape the issues I encountered with the men I loved.

Thinking about my joyful experiences growing up with my mother, there were many moments that brought a smile to my face. As a child, I spent my summers at the family camp on Belgrade Lake. With four cottages sitting one right next to one another, the Noel/Martin compound was a child's summer dream. There was always someone to play with and something being cooked to perfection on the grill. The sweet smell of barbecued chicken was a scent I would never forget.

Camp days comprised of swimming, rain or shine; playing games with my cousins; and paddle boat rides to the corner cove filled with clear water and the softest sand your feet would ever touch. When there were down times in the afternoons, we would all pile into the family boat to water ski, tube, or just cruise, letting the breeze whip our hair into new styles. Camp life was a sweet symphony of summer laughter, love, and family.

Besides our carefree lake life, my mom and I made the hour-and-a-half drive to the beach at least a couple times before August's end, and spending time at the ocean was perhaps my favorite summer activity. We would create endless games of seek and find with the colorful seashells and sea glass that had made their way ashore. I enjoyed watching the waves grow tall before crashing over my tanned feet as I played chase with the trailing water.

As I grew older, I spent more time with friends, and I joined family camping trips with my closest confidants. I loved cooking s'mores while their dads told us scary stories under the night sky. No matter which family I traveled with to a secret spot in the forest, every trip unfolded in the same beautiful way: logs burning on an open fire, pink cotton-candy skies dissolving in the dark of the night, and fireflies lighting the way back to our tent after mind-rattling ghost tales.

After the brief summers, the long cold winters consisted of sledding, skiing, and more. Sunday mornings were ice skating lessons, which then dissolved into roller-skating around the house in my dance costumes, listening to Janet Jackson. I imagined I was a famous figure skater, shaking up the ice rink with my slick moves on the living room floor. The wind lifted me high as I twisted and turned to perform my triple axel for the judges. The lingering aroma of scented candles and of mujaddara, a tasty dish of lentils, rice, fried onions, and garlic cooking on the stove, completed the perfect Sunday afternoon at home.

As I got older, unpleasant happenings trickled in little by little. I noticed more people looking at me everywhere I went. In my predominately white town, I didn't look like everyone else with their perfect peach-toned skin. And to make matters worse, I looked nothing like my mother!

I could feel the speculating heads turn, watching me with her waiting in line at stores or as we dined in restaurants. Many would ask if I was adopted. After that, I'd wake up after a long night's rest, wishing I had straight hair, pale skin, and blue eyes just like my mom.

As a teenager, I felt the wobble of what people perceived me to be, and that I somehow fell short of their ethnic expectations. There were times I felt I had to choose a color to represent, which was hard because I just wanted to be me. I wanted to love the music, clothes, and hairstyle that I chose and not base the decision on my skin color.

I started hating what I looked like. I slicked back my hair as much as I could, carrying a squirt bottle and brush with me to all of my classes. I would sneak a spritz or two while the teachers' backs were turned to eliminate any post-shower frizz. Usually, the teacher would catch me on my second spritz and take my styling tools away until the end of the period. I felt naked sitting there, armed with nothing but my fingers and spit to help tame the wild hair that God and my father had given me.

Whenever I hated my reflection, my mother would tell me to love all of myself regardless of what I thought people saw in me and to try not to compare myself to others. But I hated feeling like the sore thumb that stuck out. I *was* different with my frizzy, out-of-control hair and skin that was light brown during the winter and even darker in the summer. When you're a kid, all you want is to fit in, and when you're the one yellow Starburst in a package of all pink, it can raise havoc with your self-confidence.

In order to compensate, I started dressing like the characters in my favorite movie, *Clueless*. The gang and I, a fearless group of ten girls I had bonded with in the fourth grade, started shopping at Contempo Casual, just like Cher and Dion did in the popular film. We arrived at school dressed to kill in short skirts, knee-highs, and chunky platform shoes, and often our teachers sent us to the office, where the principal told us to go home and change. Soon, getting dressed in the morning became a game of what skirt length slid *just* under the dress code's radar.

The vibrant girls I clung to helped to create many memories of my childhood; they were my lifesavers in a sea of adolescent uncertainty. I loved the girls and was fortunate to find them after leaving a private Catholic school whose strict standards of academics I had failed to meet.

At age twelve, I was diagnosed with learning disabilities. After many years of feeling stupid because I didn't understand simple math and retained nothing I read, it was a relief when the doctor told me I was smart but learned differently than my friends. I struggled with reading comprehension and spelling, as I couldn't grasp the correct letters to form the word I was trying to construct. Sometimes, I would go to write a sentence and sit there staring at the paper, not knowing which letters went where in the next word.

In my rush to spell everything correctly before I forgot it, my penmanship was sloppy. I also had a tough time holding my pen or pencil the correct way, which only added to the messiness of the work I turned in. I was usually told to rewrite it. Sometimes the third or fourth attempt looked worse than the first. Frustrated by my lack of progress, the teachers would turn me away, letting me know my final grade would be less than stellar.

As for math, I couldn't produce a sum, let alone an equation, no matter how hard I tried to figure it out. I could calculate simple addition and subtraction by counting on my fingers or doing it the long way. As for division and multiplication, they were the devil. My teachers would call on me to answer questions, and I would just freeze, embarrassed that whatever I was about to guess would cause an uproar of laughter among my classmates.

To top off all the learning challenges, I couldn't sit still for the life of me. Fidgety and forever in movement, my body did not know calm. My mind and body were constantly running, which made it hard to sit quietly in class.

When the verdict came in from the well-known child psychologist who evaluated me, she concluded that in addition to the other academic ailments that plagued me, I also suffered from ADHD/ADD. Back then, the genuineness of the hyperactivity diagnosis was still under discussion by teachers. Some teachers were more patient with me than others, but despite my hyper body and lack of simple understanding my friends loved me just the same.

It felt great to have a good powerful circle of friends, but as we grew older, we became more daring in our choices. Like the time I freshly turned fourteen and skipped out on the bowling alley to attend a popular party with a couple of girlfriends and wound up getting arrested!

When the police were called in response to an angry neighbor's complaint about loud noises coming from the condo next door, they arrived to find a bunch of underage kids drinking and smoking. One of my girlfriends was able to escape the dilemma, running close to two miles home. My other friend and I weren't so lucky.

After calling our parents to ask them to pick us up from the police station, the remaining fifteen attendees, including me, were hauled off in cop cars and booked on charges for underage drinking. They later dropped my charges because of my writing a two-page essay for young juveniles to read as part of community service. Though I rebelled from time to time, as much as I tried to tango with the idea that I could simply swap feeling racially out of place with being a teen misfit, my love of sports would pull me back into place when I needed it to.

Sports were important to me, and I was proud of my athleticism. I took part in every seasonal sport my mom could fit into my busy schedule: tap, jazz, ballet, gymnastics, track and field, tennis, ice skating, basketball, and soccer. I was certainly well-rounded, but basketball and soccer were my favorite sports, and I lived and breathed them.

Although my basketball coach always showed me love, he could be stern, and he pushed me to be my best. I appreciated that, because he made me feel important to the team, as if the game wouldn't be the same if I weren't playing. He always looked at me when he offered new ways to improve my game, and he had a way of making me want to play better, not just for the team and the "big win," but for him because I wanted to show him I was paying attention and learning.

As for soccer, though I was one of their best players, I never got the playing time I felt I deserved. Other players, who were neither as fast nor as accurate when it came time to steal the ball, played more than I did. I think it was a socioeconomic thing. There was always a strong vibe that my mother and I, in one way or another, were less than equal and it showed in the amount of game time I received with travel soccer and high school soccer in particular.

My mother's sacrifice in accepting a smaller check in order to be an involved single parent meant we lived in a much smaller house than the other girls on the team. We still went on vacations, and I had the most sought-after toys, the coolest clothes, and new gear every sports season, but our differences were quietly evident, whether or not anyone wanted to admit it.

My mom and I lived in a small, cozy, two-bedroom apartment until I was sixteen, before moving into a small ranch of our own. The house was perfect, with a big backyard, a cool bedroom in the basement, and a beautiful neighborhood filled with inviting neighbors. I was grateful for our upgrade. It was close to the high school, which meant that the days I accidentally overslept, my morning math teacher would let my classmate leave school to come pick me up.

Even with our improved living situation, a part of me still experienced prejudice from some of the more affluent parents on the travel teams I played on. Some parents were great, kind, and welcoming, but others thumbed their noses at us for being less affluent than they were.

When varsity soccer tryouts came in high school, I was one of a few freshman suckers who had to play on both the junior varsity and freshman team. Same thing happened my sophomore year too. Only this time, it was junior varsity and varsity that I bounced between. It was hard because, by that time, I was becoming a young woman and dealing with normal teenage depression and rebellion. Like most pubescent teens, I found high school was emotionally difficult, but feeling shunned from participating in the sport I loved most was heartbreaking.

After a season-ending injury my sophomore year—a hip muscle torn right off the bone—I decided to hang it up. At the beginning of my junior year, the varsity coach begged me to reconsider, insisting that my team needed me. Unable to admit the real reason I would never play again, I politely declined and told him I was taking up dance again, though I never did. I couldn't tell him that my love for soccer had died because I wasn't recognized or given enough playing time, and it was all about social status. I wanted to insist that I was better than the handful of girls who played more than me, but I didn't have the heart to tell him he too had fallen victim to the politics of kids' sports.

It broke my heart to leave behind the sport I had played at age four and excelled at consistently as I grew. But I couldn't stand watching someone else who didn't even like the sport play because their father made six figures, or was on the school board, or was friends with all the right people. I just wanted to play the game, and I felt I was being unfairly sidelined. The only things that would have saved me were a stepdad, a spacious house, and a mother who made twice what she was earning. So I pushed down my rising anger and swallowed my resentment.

Another unpleasant childhood memory that made fitting in uncomfortable was learning about Black History month. It was brutal! As one of four ethnically diverse students at the small public school I attended, it was painful to sit and listen to how my ancestors had suffered. I could feel my classmates' eyes beaming through me like a laser, looking for an awkward reaction as the teacher read about slavery, whippings, and the Underground Railroad. I felt like I had a flashing arrow hovering above my head pointed downward, highlighting the only African American in the room.

There's nothing like an entire month of learning, dedicated to why and where skin color differences originated, to remind you you're different. I hated knowing what so many souls went through simply because of the color of their skin. The idea of being captured by colonists, then chained, sold, and "owned" made me sick. I never understood how anyone could think that they owned another person by "color rights"; how anyone could whip and torture a human being because they were born beautiful yet different in the eyes of strangers.

I couldn't very well change the circumstances of history or the planned academics for the month of February, but there were other moments growing up where I felt purposely singled out because of the color of my skin. Like the boy who called me "Blacky" when I was six, and an even more painful incident on my first day of high school.

Happy that we had completed our first day of ninth grade together, my friends and I were giddily walking home as we giggled about boys and potential love interests. Kicking stray pebbles with the tips of our shoes, we felt the fleet of upperclassmen's cars zoom by us as they sped off down the side street. Just as the train of metal hand-me-downs came to a halt, all waiting their turn to pull out onto the main road, a small Saab slowed down just enough for us to hear what they had to say as they kept driving.

At the top of their lungs, they screamed, "Nigger!" I was hurt and horrified! My face red with humiliation, I tried to shake off the degrading shout-out the best I could. My friends didn't know what to say, and neither did I, so we just kept walking. It scared me to go to school the next day, but I had no choice. I also knew it probably wouldn't be the last time I would encounter racial slurs, so just like the other uncomfortable moments, I pushed it down deep inside, with no intention of dealing with it . . . ever.

Despite feeling singled out during Black History month and by the few racial intolerants I encountered, overall, my school experience was pleasant. I was well liked by others and had an array of friends. My mother always told me to make friends with everyone, and I did my best.

My teachers liked me as well, with one exception, a high school English teacher who had a way of singling me out and making me feel as though I were stupid. Before I knew it, I was getting kicked out of his classes regularly. After his degrading, inappropriate comments to my mother during a parent–teacher conference, she demanded school officials remove me from his class.

Fortunately for me, they placed me in a caring, supportive classroom environment with a teacher who helped me to see my true talent for writing. I could explore and reveal my feelings with the words I chose to put on paper. Using a computer to help with my learning disabilities, I blossomed under her encouragement.

As juniors and seniors, we had the option of taking a trade class like carpentry, auto body, cooking, or childcare. I was different from most girls and signed up for carpentry one year and auto body the other. I loved building houses and fixing up cars. I felt superior as a girl, working just as hard as the guys. Sometimes I would even show them up with my brick-laying skills, shingling expertise, and precise welding.

I jumped at the chance to enter a writing competition open to all the vocational school students in Maine. The judges cried as I read my memorized speech about how I had gotten to where I was in life and worked through the things that had happened along the way. In that moment, seeing tears stream down their faces, I understood the power of the written word and was thirsty for more. When it came time for the closing ceremony after a three-day extravaganza, joy overwhelmed me as I heard my name called over the loudspeaker.

I joined the winner's circle, barely able to breathe as I stood there tall on the podium to receive my silver medal. I didn't want to move as I climbed down. I wanted to relive the moment again and again. And in a flash, I thought of the English teacher who had treated me like an unwanted child and realized that if it hadn't been for our conflicts, I wouldn't have met Ms. Z; I wouldn't have met the woman who set fire to my hidden talent.

I pressed *stop* on the play button of my life. Lack of learning about self-love or feeling loved as a child wasn't my issue. Moving on from how others had made me feel was. As I played over the old tapes in my mind, I saw a fine line of resentment toward the uppity folks, nosey strangers, and racist schoolmates who knowingly or unwittingly clarified that I was different from them.

It was no longer necessary for me to hide the leftover emotional impact of the accident, that still had a "cause and effect" on my day-to-day activity. It was there, and I knew it, but in hindsight, I could see where I still carried feelings of bitterness from the behavior of others I had dwelled on when I was younger.

I sometimes felt stuck in the same small town raising two children of my own: my son, whose skin was deep like mine, and my daughter, who looked nothing like me with her light brown hair, blue eyes, and light complexion. Deep down, I worried that my childhood experiences would begin all over again and trickle down to my children.

The push and pull between always feeling that I was neither "white" enough nor "black" enough terrified me that my children might take the same blows to their self-confidence that I had; that the same name-callers would shout out to them.

It was clear the chip on my shoulder was not only present, but still growing, collecting other grudges along with it. My refusal to let go of uncomfortable circumstances, past and present, was the broken foundation trying to hold steady my flimsy house of cards built by unhappy memories and hurts caused by others.

I was still letting things that I had experienced years ago dictate who I was and how I handled discomfort with others. Anytime something didn't go my way or I felt like I was being shunned somehow, I added to a mental hit list of people, unable to repair the broken links between us. Whether I completely extracted myself from the circumstances or the person, I allowed the hurt to fester and brew, attracting more things to bottle up.

Considering this in the reflection of Louise Hay's teachings, I realized it was best to continue reading despite the awkward childhood reflections it had brought up, and so I did.

Regarding self-healing, Louise stated that in order to let go of the past that tortured us, we must first forgive. Shifting our attitude and living in the present moment were also keys to living the way we wanted to now. Adamant that all dis-ease started from the inability to forgive and let go, she said one simply needed to be "willing" to release what held them captive, and the Universe would handle the rest.

She shared her own personal story of surviving cervical cancer, noting it was no surprise her cancer had grown where it had. In addition to being raped by a neighbor when she was only five, she had suffered abuse, both physical and sexual, during her childhood before finally fleeing her family home at age fifteen. Frequently told that she "asked for" the sexual assault, she spent years fearful that her assailant would come back to harm her again.

Louise knew through her work that cancer resulted from deep-seated resentment that had festered in the body, eating away at what health remained, and she understood that the inability to release the anger from her childhood had caused her dis-ease. She got to work and began healing herself. Faced with the idea of repeated surgeries if the cancer recurred, she knew that if she released it mentally and had surgery to remove the growth, she could heal completely. She also knew that she would need to love herself more than she had been loved as a child and stop belittling herself.

Wasting no time, she visited health food stores and purchased books on cancer. She started seeing a therapist to help free the trapped emotions from her childhood. In addition, she saw a reflexologist and a nutritionist. Six months into her personal treatment and healing journey, she discovered she was cancer free, and without surgery. Sometimes, she said, the biggest tragedies faced in life can also be the best thing to happen to us, and what she learned during that time caused her to look at and value life in a new light.

I immediately thought of all the things I had to release. I thought about the guilt I carried toward the people I had hurt and the things I had been ashamed of doing. I thought about the times I had been offended or hurt by someone else and the grudges I held against those who hurt me recently, as well as many years ago. In fact, on my bad days, I might still bring up what they had done, thinking that shoving it in their face to remind them of their actions would somehow make them feel the hurt they had caused in me, but it never did. It only made me hurt more.

I could see how hanging on to old baggage was disrupting me, both mentally and physically. After reading how Louise connected body issues and the inability to release old emotions, I knew I was finally ready to let go. Ready to release all the times the words and actions of others had saddened me. Using positive affirmations and learning new thought patterns, I would help save me from myself and the mess I had made of my life.

I took a physical inventory. Though I was basically healthy, I experienced sporadic eczema, stiff joints, and chronic back and neck pain. I knew the back and neck pain was a result of a sledding accident at sixteen, but I hadn't the slightest clue why the other bothersome ailments had surfaced.

Careening down what town folk referred to as "the crippla"—Mainer slang for "crippler"—my friend and I took a heavy haul off a homemade jump and lived to tell about it. Buried deep beneath the snow sat an old, discarded wooden door waiting to launch daring victims off its daunting lift. We hopped on an inner tube together and began the descent down the hill with a hard push from friends. As soon as we hit the jump, all I heard was silence as we floated in the air while doing a backward somersault. I woke up at the bottom of the hill with bells ringing loudly in my ears and friends screaming my name and calling for an ambulance.

I spent the next three days in the ICU of our local hospital with a concussion, possibly torn spleen, and major snow rash all over my face. I had landed on my head and neck, with my friend on top of me, and then skid down the icy slope, tearing off large pieces of facial skin along with my earring.

The doctors said the fall from the launch was like being thrown seventy feet from a car crash. I was lucky I hadn't been hurt worse.

More than a decade later, the crash still haunted me. Sometimes I could just move the wrong way or sleep in a weird position, and my neck would be stiff for weeks. Or something as simple as a sneeze would throw out my upper back for days, with sharp spasms shooting up and down my neck every time I tilted my head. I often considered going back on the muscle relaxants my doctor had prescribed me years ago when I was experiencing almost daily discomfort.

The eczema seemed to come mostly during warmer months, raging like a tropical storm and leaving me with itchy patches and a full-body red rash. As for the constant pain stemming from the joint in my thumb, I often wondered if I had early signs of rheumatoid arthritis or fibromyalgia. As both my grandmother and mother both suffered from arthritis, I wondered if I were next in line for the crippling illness.

Since I knew my self-diagnosis always resulted in a worst-case scenario, I tried to imagine what Louise would say about my bodily ailments. I had often wondered what induced them, and now that I was armed with the favorite book of my dear friend and the brilliant knowledge of Louise Hay, I soon devised solutions. I flipped back to her illness dictionary and started thumbing through the pages for the current dis-eases in my body that I just couldn't seem to shake.

Starting with eczema, I drew my finger along the soft pages until I found my problem listed in the column. When I saw the problematic cause was listed as "Breathtaking antagonism. Mental eruptions," my stomach dropped. I swallowed hard at the word "mental" and could feel a slight rise in tension with the familiarity of the cause.

As much as I hated to admit it, I could, at times, become so consumed with paranoia stemming from anxious thoughts that I often felt like I needed a team of psychologists to put out the flames. As a thought pattern to induce healing, Louise listed the following: "Harmony and peace, love and joy surround me and indwell me. I am safe and secure."

It was easy enough to repeat, but I understood that I had severely depleted my feelings of safety after the car accident in 2013. Reading her approach that it was, in fact, safe to live brought me ease. It was as if I needed to hear it from a complete stranger in order for it to register.

Eager to move on to the next, I quickly flipped backward to the B's and looked for the word "back." Listed in three parts—lower, middle and upper—the part that always bothered me most was my upper. As I reviewed the emotional cause, "Lack of emotional support. Feeling unloved. Holding back love," I thought of how spot-on she was in determining the driving force behind my back pain.

My lack of trust in others was responsible for why I struggled to turn, breathe, or even wipe my backside when the spasms began. The towering wall of protection I had built was constricting my ability to let others love and support me the way I deserved. Moving my finger across to the new thought, I chuckled as I read what was listed: "I love and approve of myself. Life supports and loves me."

It all made sense. I was afraid to be vulnerable and unable to accept love without thinking that the person would hurt me. Even more so, I often played victim and claimed no one understood what I was feeling. I was almost afraid to read what the other physical problems represented.

I assumed the neck problem would be similar to the back because it was all connected. But my mouth fell open when I read the problem behind it: "Refusing to see other sides of a question. Stubbornness, inflexibility."

I quickly shut the book and threw it down on the couch beside me. I was angry. Angry for making things worse over the past six years. Angry at all the stupid things I hadn't let go of, and angry that my stubbornness was now manifesting itself in the aches and pains that circulated my body.

I pulled myself together and ordered my fingers to open the book back up. If I wanted things to change, quitting and hiding wouldn't get me where I wanted to be. Despite feeling embarrassed by my self-inflicted misery, in that moment of weakness on the couch, I saw strength hidden beneath the ruins. I firmly reached over and grabbed the book, opened it back up to where I had left off, and read the new thought pattern to resolve my stubbornness: "It is with flexibility and ease that I see all sides of an issue. There are endless ways of doing things and seeing things. I am safe."

I thought others were in the wrong because they couldn't see where they were coming from. I shook my head, knowing how silly I had acted for all those years. I had literally lived "my way or the highway." Now I felt ashamed of how I had treated those closest to me during disagreements and understood that it was an emotion I needed to feel in order to truly see how my behavior affected others.

Bravely turning to the last of my pesky little ailments, there at the top of the page was "Fingers," followed by a different cause and resolution for every phalange. Thumb issues represented "Intellect and worry," and the four-word sentence to resolve it was, "My mind is at peace." I could easily override the idea that the sharp pain that kept me from opening jars and had me struggling to turn doorknobs with four simple words seemed silly compared to the amount of courage it would take to believe in the healing words.

Although I suspected the thumb would be the hardest to heal mentally, since my worst habit was worrying, I enjoyed the prospect of being worry free rather than filled with anxieties.

I was ready to move on, knowing which affirmations would heal me. I shut the book again, ready and willing to do whatever it took to provide my body with the wellness it deserved. Calming my mind, I told my consciousness that I was healthy *now* and would continue to heal through new thought patterns.

After thanking the pains that sporadically greeted me for not being more severe, I memorized the affirmations. I knew that if I truly focused on the suggested new thought patterns to heal the minor issues I had now, I would restore my body and it would remain healthy through continuing affirmations.

I chanted the mantras repeatedly aloud. As soon as I had spoken the new thought pattern about fifteen times, I started to hear and feel what I was saying. Not just the sound of my voice speaking.

With my eyes closed, I listened to the tone of my voice. I listened to the reality it spoke and the belief that backed its meaning. I wanted more than anything to change, but most importantly, I wanted to be the best I could for my family because they were the ones who had to deal with my anxieties. Taking in deep breaths followed with long exhales, I paced my mind with my words and envisioned my life of wellness.

Over the next few months, I opened the book up from time to time and learned new concepts about attracting money, loving my bills, and planting new seeds for what I preferred to grow. I was working hard on my affirmations daily and slowing down my negative thoughts in the process. Before I knew it, my eczema had cleared up completely, my neck was flexible as ever, and I didn't have to ask my family to open jars for me any longer.

Reaching out to my dear friend, I thanked her and shared my love and appreciation for Louise's book just as I had for Rhonda's. I had a stronger sense of responsibility and a better connection with my mind and body. However, I still had had no takers for the newly revised manuscript. Out of the hundred queries I had sent, only two agents replied. One told me to lengthen the book, and the other told me to lengthen it and to make sure that my manuscript was a bit more "polished" before resubmitting it. All the others had sent automated rejection slips.

When I looked again at the 36,000-word memoir, it appalled me to see a shit ton of misspellings I had missed. My lack of professionalism embarrassed me, and I didn't know what to do next. The prospect of revising and expanding the memoir was daunting and joyless. I had already rewritten the book twice and thought it was amazing.

When I shared my frustration with my dear friend, she explained it was all a part of the journey and that, for whatever reason, the book just wasn't ready to be published yet. When she suggested I reach out to her medium, Gina Self, for a directional reading, it seemed like the next logical thing to do.

I sent a text message to Gina asking to schedule a phone session. Gina lived in the beautiful state of Colorado, just as my dear friend did, 2,129 miles away from the "Vacationland" I called home. She told me to set up an appointment through the scheduling link on her website, so I immediately pulled up the page to learn who Gina Self was.

Born with the special gift of intuition, Gina had worked under many mediums from around the world. Besides being a medium, psychic, medical intuitive, and certified Reiki II healer, she was also an energy healer and psychic investigator. She loved tarot and astrology and took her work and the lifetime process of dedication to her special gift seriously.

At age three, Gina had begun to see and hear spirits. One night when she was five, a "shadowed man" walking back and forth down the hall frightened her. He spoke to her, letting her know he was there to protect her, but that anytime she felt afraid of the other spirits, she should pretend there was a light bulb shining brightly above her head, and then nothing could harm her.

By age twelve, Gina was alone, raising herself. It was at this point that she became aware of her intuition. She knew who was trustworthy and who wasn't. Using her gift in lieu of a parental figure, Gina kept herself safe from danger.

It wasn't until Gina was seventeen, driving in her Spitfire, that she heard the voice again of the friendly spirit that guided her back when she was five. She hit black ice while crossing a bridge, and time stopped. In that moment, she heard the helpful voice guiding her to take her hands off the steering wheel, hold on to the bottom of her seat, and lean over to her right. Complying with the voice, she did so mere seconds before the car flipped over, landing in the bed of a dry creek. With only a few bruises and some hair loss, Gina had survived with the help of her unseen guide. If she hadn't listened, the totaled car would have decapitated her.

Moved to tears by her story, I could see that Gina was not only gifted and special, but strong. Raising herself and overcoming obstacles in life, Gina never hesitated to fulfill what she knew was her life purpose, helping others with her gift of intuition.

I wondered if I had once again given up too easily with the manuscript.

I clicked through the times I wanted on her scheduling page and hit send. I was thrilled to talk to the reputable and popular medium and was determined to be open-minded and calm when the day came for us to speak.

Two weeks later, in the comfort of my living room, I answered the scheduled phone call from Gina Self with shaking hands and a rapid heartbeat. But her energetic voice immediately washed away any waves of hesitation. As she greeted me and filled me in on how the call would play out, I became more relaxed with every word she spoke.

I had booked a thirty-minute session, and the time flew. I felt I could talk to her for hours about everything in life. Gina was the new friend I never knew I needed, who told me things about my life and personality that she had no way of knowing. The strength of her gift fascinated me and knew I made the right decision by calling.

With just a few minutes left, I explained I had written a manuscript for a second time, and it had been rejected by everyone I had sent it to. When I asked if I should move in a new direction with my writing, perhaps trying out a genre like romance, she quickly replied no, that my writing gift was supposed to help people, and I needed to make the book longer. She felt I already queried the person who would help me get published, so I should go back to work and resubmit.

After thanking her for her guidance, I hung up, grateful that my dear friend had brought another piece of goodness into my life. But her assertion puzzled me that my book agent was among the hundred that I had already reached out to, and I wondered if I could actually write the book a third time.

Painful as it had been to relive the traumatic memories I had written about, I wasn't sure if I was strong enough to do it all over again. I was five weeks into my second-to-last term at Purdue Global and considered if I even had time to write between the ten-page term papers and the series of discussion questions that needed to be researched and answered every week.

Deep into learning about the minds of serial killers, other criminals, and a variety of deranged crimes in pursuit of my criminal justice degree, I was hesitant to revisit something that brought up the parts of me I was trying to forget and move past. I found that studying the dark underside of society made me worry about more things.

So what did I do after being advised by a talented psychic? I decided halfway through my school term to write a romance novel. Plugging away at the computer, I poured out pulsating details of lovers who had just met and whose romance took a suspenseful turn after facing a daring dilemma involving secrecy and cover-up. It took less than ten weeks, and I was shocked at my productivity. I had produced quality work while spending five of those ten weeks studying, researching, and writing lengthy term papers. Astonished that I had cranked out a sixty-thousand-word novel in under three months, I knew I could publish several books a year with the right agent, editor, and publisher on my team.

This time, the editing had to be near perfect, so I reached out to my stepmother for help. Sherry had taught English to children in Peru for five years, as well as editing the resumes of several coworkers. With a keen eye for errors, she was perfect for the job. Since we shared a different bond as stepmother and stepdaughter, I was comfortable enough for an avid romance reader like her to read my steamy novel.

We spent countless hours over the next month and a half, sending edits back and forth until the book was perfect. When the time came to submit, I was confident in what we accomplished and so grateful for her help.

Then I began researching book agents again, who were a good fit for the novel. I took my time, just as before, submitting only to those whom I sensed would best represent it. Armed with a strong query letter, I sent out numerous submissions over the next four weeks. I felt positive about the *action* I had taken to get things done quickly and knew it was only a matter of time before I heard something back.

Pushing aside the thought of being turned down again, I proactively told myself to "reject rejection" just as Jack Canfield had done. So, while waiting once again for feedback from book agents, I shifted gears, placing my focus on the expansion of my mind.

As I searched for new information, I was like a well-oiled machine sucking up data, and for the first time in my life, I saw the dreams I was destined for and knew they were obtainable. I finished two books in less than six months after not writing for years, and all it had taken was encouragement from complete strangers and an open mind.

The books and people who were feeding my hungry mind with facts of natural laws and a fresh approach to thinking were changing my life in ways I never knew even existed. Their wisdom filled my soul with a new yearning, a drug I never knew I needed.

One day I stumbled upon a 1950s TV production about the keys to success on Amazon Prime, produced by a man named Napoleon Hill. Born into poverty in the late 1880s, Hill was just fifteen when he began his career as a writer, working as a reporter for a small paper in Virginia.

In 1908, they assigned him to interview a list of successful men and report back their stories in a series of articles. One of them was Andrew Carnegie, an American industrialist turned philanthropist, who had been a major player in the steel industry. After twenty years, he sold Carnegie Steel to banker John Pierpont Morgan for $480 million. Carnegie later gave away more than $350 million in philanthropy work.

During the intriguing interview, the steel mogul became quite smitten with the young writer's skill and encouraged him to make an abrupt change in his life. Believing the steps to success could be documented in a simple formula, Carnegie told Hill that he should set out and interview five hundred millionaires to come up with the perfect formula for success.

Hill took on Carnegie's challenge and changed the lives of many through sharing the common denominator to personal achievement. After his accomplishment with Carnegie, he took his findings and went on to publish many books, the most popular of which, *Think and Grow Rich*, sold over a hundred million copies.

After publishing various self-help books, Hill formed a partnership with W. Clement Stone, an American businessman, author, and philanthropist. Stone, mentioned in *The Secret*, by Jack Canfield, who had worked for him, was the driving force behind the shift in Canfield's life.

High on anticipation and the connections I was finding, I watched as the first video of *Napoleon Hill's Master Key* loaded on the small screen of my iPhone. With its eerie introductory music, I felt as if I were being pulled into a time warp, acknowledging the era of fifties television. Standing in an office with books surrounding him, Hill exuded confidence as he pleasantly greeted his viewers, standing up from the single chair behind his heavy desk.

I was excited I had found something much older than the reading material and YouTube videos I had been watching. I appreciated what Hill and Stone were trying to do, because back then, it was ground-breaking material. The fact that the series even existed showed two things: longevity behind the Law of Attraction and a strong sense of commitment by the people who taught it, regardless of public backlash.

Unleashing his philosophical discoveries in an instructional, easy-to-follow process, Hill outlined exactly what one must do to get the peace of mind and the material wealth that one desired. If his listeners would relax and leave their problems behind them, Hill promised to teach the principles that made up the "master key to success" to those who were *ready*.

Speaking calmly and with confidence to support his beliefs, Hill stated that psychologists had found a natural law that underlies the basis of success: "Whatever the mind can conceive and believe, the mind can achieve." I liked the simplicity of the intriguing catchphrase.

Hill talked of how he first heard of the natural law that allowed everyone to "write their own price tag in life" from Andrew Carnegie, who had taught him that the power of the mind was astronomical, and through controlled thought, anything was achievable. Carnegie further said that the ability to control the mind was a gift given to us by the creator, and that fretting about things like poverty would only attract more of it.

I listened, spellbound, as Hill shared another of Carnegie's intriguing insights, that at birth we were all given two envelopes, and the choice was ours if we wanted to succeed or not. Hill intently described the contents of the two envelopes.

Envelope one contained an abundance of blessings available if one grasped the ability to direct their own mind to the things they wanted: strong health, peace of mind, a fulfilling career, freedom from worry and fear, a positive attitude, and ample material riches.

The second envelope contained the penalties one would succumb to if they failed to take control over their mind: worry, illness, fear, indecisiveness, doubt, frustration, and poverty. In addition to this list, he also added most of the seven deadly sins: greed, jealousy, envy, hatred, and anger.

I considered the envelope I had chosen before my dear friend interceded months ago. With my heart beating fast, excited that I was now taking the steps to leave behind the second envelope, I sat patiently like an excellent student, waiting for my next assignment.

Hill pointed out that every success starts with a *definite major purpose* and emphasized that the first principle required a *clear* idea of what was wanted in life. After suggesting that viewers grab a notebook, he instructed them to write exactly what they desired for success and what it would take to get there. Next, he wanted them to write precisely what they planned to give in return for having realized their desire. I was struck by the similarity between Hill's teaching and what Rhonda and her team had said for manifesting one's desired success . . . *clarity*.

I set my phone down and hurried upstairs to unearth the journal that languished somewhere in the sea of shoes at the bottom of my closet. Tossing my favorite Nikes aside and stacking my collection of strappy sandals, one on top of the other, I saw how much I had. Mounds of clothes hanging low from the closet rod reminded me that Carnegie had given away most of his fortune. I thought about what I might give back and how amazing it would feel. I recalled my dream of one day helping kids in the public school system. I had always given outgrown or unused clothes away, but once I really felt the real motive behind giving—that it wasn't just about clearing out a closet—I thought about ways to turn a closet purge into an easy way to help others.

With success from my definite major purpose, I would create a foundation that provided gently used clothes to school children. People could collect their unwanted clothes and leave them outside their house for easy, curbside pickup. Many school-aged children suffered from poverty, poor parenting, and abuse. With shoes too small and clothes dirty with last week's stains, the kids were anything but presentable. Besides being unkempt and underfed, it was a wonder how some of them made it to the bus most mornings.

These children were expected to come to school and learn for seven hours a day, five days a week, despite the dysfunction in their home environments. In addition to living in hardship, they sometimes looked like they hadn't showered in days and their hair hadn't been cut professionally . . . ever! Something as simple as gently used clothing could make a kid's confidence grow as high as Jack's beanstalk.

Delighted that I now had a clear idea of how I intended to give back, I finally unearthed the journal. With a pen still stuck in its metal column, I slid it up and out of the coiled tube that bound the book together and anxiously bit the cap off. Holding the plastic covering in my mouth, I flipped to the second page, and jotted my idea—CARE FOR KIDS—in big, blue letters. Ideas flooded through me. Care for Kids would not only provide donated clothes and shoes to local public schools. It would also have different branches stemming from it like Cuts for Kids, a program that would work with local salons and barber shops several times a year to provide free professional haircuts so these kids would look their best.

Funding would come from large businesses and individual donors looking to give back to the community, supporting a nonprofit program created to build confidence for the children who would shape the future of the town and perhaps the world.

I sat back, resting against the frame of the door, and absorbed what had just happened. I hadn't even gotten through the first principle, and I was already attracting inspiration. I flipped back to the first page and wrote my definite major purpose. Pressing down hard on the pen to release as much ink as I could, I wrote in large letters: TO BE A BEST-SELLING AUTHOR OF MANY SELF-HELP BOOKS.

I shut the journal, hopped up, and ran back downstairs, leaping off the last step, and jumping down like a child at play. I was excited, thinking of how one day my philanthropy work would positively change the experience of school for underprivileged kids. I thanked the Universe for the guidance of my thoughts, sat back down on the couch, and listened to the tail end of the lesson.

Hill asked people to repeat their definite major purpose and what they intended to do with their success many times a day and concluded with a prayer to be humbly spoken with it: "Oh, Divine Providence, I ask not for more riches, but more wisdom with which to accept and use wisely the riches I received at birth, in the form of the power to control and direct my mind to whatever ends I desire."

I tried to memorize the prayer and wondered how long it had been since I last prayed. I prayed mostly when I needed something, and the idea of praying daily in thanks and for the guidance to use the wisdom of my mind seemed pretty unconventional. I liked that it differed from the traditional prayers I knew. In fact, it was the complete opposite of the basic prayers taught to me in catechism class as a child.

While I waited for the next episode to load, I laughed at the realization that I actually had quiet time to myself to watch a series. Normally busy, always hoping for a moment of solitude in my day, suddenly, I had time that seemed to have come out of nowhere. Clearly, the Universe was moving things around, and to my benefit.

I lay down to stretch out as I rested my head on the arm of the sofa and allowed Hill's teachings to greet me once again. The next principle he discussed was the *Mastermind* principle, which involved working with two or more people toward the goal of the intended, definite major purpose.

Referring to it as a "Mastermind alliance," Hill stressed the importance of forming a bond with people who supported the definite major purpose, so that the one seeking achievement could draw on the helpful skills, knowledge, and personal experience of the others.

Each segment lasted less than thirteen minutes, and I was gliding along smoothly and with no interruptions. The baby was sleeping, and my oldest was playing, keeping himself occupied, which was a rare occasion.

As Hill laid out the rest of the principles precisely, I swiftly began taking notes, scribbling them down as he spoke of the formula that had changed his life.

1. *Habit of going the extra mile*: Going the extra mile would separate one's abilities from another's and would heavily dictate the outcome of the intended achievement.
2. *Applied faith*: Mentally shaping one's attitude in a way that washed away all fear and doubt so focus could be drawn to the desired accomplishment.
3. *Pleasing personality*: A pleasing personality would set one apart from others by showing off their favorable characteristics.
4. *Self-discipline*: Halting the urge to argue with others, self-discipline was remembering that what was pushed onto others ultimately would be pushed back.
5. *Positive mental attitude*: Starting each day with laughter and setting the brain chemistry to an exceptional level would help put one in a position for positivity.
6. *Enthusiasm*: Contagious, both good and bad, released enthusiasm would spread like dandelion seeds blown by the wind, transmitting one's vibration out into the world.
7. *Personal initiative*: The individual push to finish what was started, personal initiative placed responsibility on one to carry out their *own* definite major purpose.
8. *Learning from adversity*: Finding positivity in unwanted disappointments and failures and translating them into blessings.
9. *Creative vision*: Responsible for generating plans for the purpose through imagination, there were two types to be considered: synthetic and created.
10. *Accurate thinking*: The ability to differentiate matters of importance and unimportance. Not wasting time on insignificant issues that repelled positivity.
11. *Cosmic habit force:* A natural law sustaining the

balance of the Universe, cosmic habit force set the motion of attainment through one's habitual patterns.

I wondered how many of Hill's principles I was already using and how many principles I had yet to master. As I reflected on the steps I'd listed, I quickly realized the areas I needed to work on the most.

Sustaining a positive mental attitude definitely called for a boost. The actions of those around me could easily annoy me, and it was up to me to instead find something shiny to dig out from it, like a gemstone hidden beneath the dirt. It would take practice to see the diamond in the rough on every occasion, especially since I had a manner of reacting strongly to get my point across, and stubbornly ignoring the points of others.

I could go days without talking, using the silent treatment as a weapon and often overlooking ways to join forces and make peace with whomever I was feuding with. I loved having the last word and the way it made me feel heard . . . superior. Like I knew what I was talking about. Clearly my mental attitude toward life and others had essentially torched any possibility of a productive mindset, instead of allowing myself to remain calm and persistent.

Accurate thinking seemed to be the next extensive area that needed improvement. I had spent years focusing on trivial things that didn't serve me, and I clearly needed to break this pattern. It also tied into what Louise had said about not hanging onto things that didn't serve you, like past traumas or old anger. I had a habit of picking fights with people closest to me over ridiculous things that didn't serve either party. When I thought about what was really going on, especially in my relationships, I realized most of the time, I was wrong, and my inaccurate thinking had been at fault.

Another area that needed work was my personal traits. Mostly, I had an outgoing personality that was loud and noticeable. Stubborn when things didn't go my way, I found that my personality shifted easily with the situations that surrounded me. I was also frequently moody because of hidden anxiety.

I now understood that my presence should bring light to others and not frustration stemming from my personal problems, so anything leading to personal discomfort had to go. That included the infamous, unpleasant facial expression I took on when annoyed, as well as my sarcastic tone of voice when I experienced discomfort in conversation.

Since my behavior was a choice, I could easily change my thoughts when triggered by others. In doing so, I would alter my "unlikeable" personality traits by replacing my normal, aggressive responses with pleasant ones, regardless of the situation. Instead of producing a terrific comeback with those I bickered with occasionally, I needed to make the moment of opposition better, not worse.

I already had a sound idea of what I needed to work on and was confident in the principles I had unknowingly already achieved. For instance, I had formed a Mastermind alliance with my stepmother editing my romance novel. I had also asked the family friend who had read my mini-memoir about the correct dialogue structure. With their help and going the extra mile to crank the novel out so quickly, surely it was only a matter of time before I would start hearing from agents to represent the manuscript.

As I scanned through the rest of the principles, I knew I had most of the others under control after reading *The Secret* and *You Can Heal Your Life*. So, over the next few weeks, I worked hard at the changes I needed to make. I could feel certain parts of me shift with the increased vibration and noticed how my improved attitude was rubbing off on those around me. It was amazing to watch how a change in myself was helping those that I loved most: my family.

However, despite my efforts, I still hadn't heard from any agent about my manuscripts. I didn't understand. I had been actively working on all of Hill's principles, even improving on the ones I had already been doing. I was confused why I hadn't seen personal evidence yet to support the things he was claiming.

When I practiced what I had learned from Rhonda's journal of dos and don'ts for intentional manifestation, I had seen results almost instantly. With Hill's principles, I wondered what I was missing or doing incorrectly. Or maybe I simply hadn't given it enough time.

I decided to let the future of my romance novel rest in the hands of the Universe. I went back to Louise's book and wondered what other areas of my life needed healing or forgiveness, whether I was subconsciously still hanging on to something that was blocking me from receiving my manifestation.

While I racked my brain, I felt it was best to occupy myself in other areas. I reached out to a close friend whom I hadn't spoken to in months, someone who had helped me out on the worst day of my life and who had also brought me in contact with the man I was currently sharing my life with.

I thought of her often, wondering how she was doing. I was sad when she moved away a couple of years earlier. People change, and friends sometimes drift apart, but I missed her and took the first step and sent her a text.

Her friendship meant a lot to me, as she had always been part of my support system at the times I needed it most. Our weekend slumber parties were full of laughter, deep conversations, and nineties hip-hop. Salmon chipotle salads and Patrón Margaritas were our favorite treats to eat and drink. She was the wind in my sail, setting me loose to roam the seas of salvation after guiding me through tumultuous waters. I cherished our friendship and how she had helped me through one of the worst times in my life after the accident.

Back then I was a complete mess, unable to make any decisions without the help from those around me, and, my oh my, how she took the brunt of my indecision, even more so than my mother. I had been so needy before my spiritual journey, it was surprising that I had any friends left. The way I complained about all the things that sucked in my life, as a result of making the same mistakes repeatedly, I was lucky they still loved me.

As I waited for her response, I was thankful for the understanding I had received in knowing how I needed to be a better friend. Friendship was about making one another better, not dumping issues I wasn't brave enough to deal with on my own on the people who cared most for me. Of course, there would be times I would need advice, but it was up to me to choose what I shared with my friends, and it was time to focus on sharing the good things, not the bad.

Forty minutes after reaching out with my text, I heard back from her. We had an honest exchange of feelings about why we hadn't been in touch and decided to catch up even more on the phone later that weekend. So when Saturday came a few days later, I discovered we were on the same spiritual journey, both learning about manifesting through the Law of Attraction. We laughed about old times and shared new tricks of changing old thought patterns that didn't serve us.

By the time we got off the phone, I was glad I had reached out. Just hearing her voice and her famous laugh that I loved so much, I was thankful for all that she had taught me. A strong mother, always going after what she wanted, she could push through her problems, which was what I admired most about her.

I wanted to share the gift of what my dear friend had shared with me, Louise Hay's *You Can Heal Your Life*. We exchanged addresses, and five days later, I received a text from her thanking me for the book. She was tickled with how beautiful the illustrations were, and I was full of joy to have given her this gift.

A few days later, I made my way to the mailbox to find something from Amazon with her return address on it. I tore off the duct tape, peeled back the corners of the cardboard, and pulled out the surprise of a lifetime. A beautiful woman named Gabrielle

Bernstein smiled kindly back at me from the jacket of her book cover. I remembered my friend referring to her books when we shared tidbits of what we had learned about manifestation. Gabrielle's teachings had now made their way to my front door.

Thrilled to discover a new book to dive into, the results of our book exchange touched me. I fanned through its pages, just as I had with *The Secret*, wondering what the best-selling book *Super Attractor* offered me. It fascinated me when I came across a section in the introduction defining the term *manic manifesting* and realized this was exactly what I had been doing. Contrary to trusting in the Universe and carrying the knowledge and tools required for the journey of spirituality, manic manifesting blocked one's own manifestations from coming to fruition. By energetically overloading on prayer and affirmations, one forgot the major game play in attracting what one wants from the Universe: tuning in to the Universe through alignment with one's actual power.

I realized within the first few pages of Gabrielle's book that I needed to find a better balance among my daily practices. I needed to ensure my faith in what I was doing through more focus on aligning with the power of the Universe, something I had inadvertently neglected to do.

I felt even more connected to Gabrielle and her book after learning some adversities she had overcome. She had beaten addiction in 2005 and was now the author of several spiritual books, which for me spoke volumes of her strength, having overcome addiction myself. After reading the first chapter, I could see how her teachings were helpful.

Her *choose again method* helped readers overcome their intrusive and negative thoughts. I dove right into her practical three-step process for shifting unwanted thoughts. The first step was recognizing the unwanted thought, and the second was forgiving it. The last step was to choose a more productive thought.

Gabrielle's method was not only simple to remember but was absolutely what I needed to move past the places I was getting stuck. Although I was learning fast and practicing what I had been taught, I still had moments of weakness when I beat myself up over my unproductive thoughts. When I learned it was okay and that I could forgive the thought before thanking it, it took a load off my shoulders.

Knowing that it happened to others and hearing Gabrielle's advice helped me to feel more at ease when the negative thoughts came. Now, instead of allowing momentum to form, I simply shifted my feelings to thoughts of recognition followed by thanks and what I chose to think of instead.

I loved Gabrielle's approach. I started watching YouTube videos of her as I did my household chores, and I found I was attracting exactly the videos I needed to deal with what was going on in my life that day.

One day, I found an interview with Gabrielle and host Lewis Howes. During the interview, I could see that she was a human being with lots of experience looking to help others who often found themselves in similar situations. It was easy to feel connected to her, which made listening that much more rewarding.

Regarding indecisiveness, she stated that when in doubt, you should always ask the Universe for signs of guidance. The Universe would deliver. Every time. If you didn't receive a sign, that was a sign as well. A sign could be anything at all, and if it was meant to be, you would receive one. Always.

I thought about this. I had always loved receiving signs of bluebirds and cardinals from loved ones who had passed. I wanted to separate my feel-good signs from those living beyond the earthly planes, so I created a list of other signs that would be of significance when asking for guidance from the Universe.

First on my personal list of go-to signs was a butterfly. I had always loved butterflies and how they were born from a cocoon, fluttering into genuine beauty after breaking free from the chrysalises that confined them. To me, butterflies represented the beauty that could shine through the ugliness I often saw wrapped around me, carrying around the weight of past traumas.

Second on my list were rainbows. Full of radiant colors, every time I saw one after a storm, I knew there was a pot of gold at the end. Rainbows signified life after adversity, which really resonated with me.

Finally, eagles, which represented a sense of bold strength in their long wingspan soaring high above the atrocities of the world. When I felt weary in moments of weakness, the eagle would stand as a sign to fly high above any issues that caused discomfort, reminding me how much strength I really carried.

Later that evening, after I had created my list of signs, I found my mind wandering while watching a movie with my partner. Triggered by a scene in the film, I quickly slipped into thoughts that didn't serve me. Then, turning to Gabrielle's choose again method, I told myself I was just doing that thing I did, and that it was okay. I forgave the thought, thanked it for setting me back on track, and chose to think again, knowing the Universe had my back.

Within seconds of coaching myself to safety, I experienced something mind-blowing when the movie I was watching gave me the biggest sign of all. I'd been unable to hear the exchange of words between the characters on screen while I was engaged in choosing again. But suddenly, a character made a statement in a firm voice, reminding me that the Universe is always with me and supporting me in magical ways.

I was shocked by what I heard. Directly after I had taken my mind to a better place, away from the negative thought trying to consume me, the Universe had responded that it was always there for support, and I had a job to do as well: to stay focused on my definite major purpose and only think thoughts that served me.

The day after my wakeup call, I felt like another shift had occurred in me while I slept. Still elated with the film quote the Universe had sent loud and clear, I felt happy about the choices I had made and put them into action to help guide me when I was confused or lost. Over the next month, I opened up all my senses to apply my personal touch to the listening ears of the Universe and was astounded by what I found. In every moment that I needed it, sometimes without even posing a question, my personal signs were coming at me left and right.

From giant rainbows beaming from cards in checkout aisles to an eagle flying fifteen feet above my car, the number of signs was shocking. I could be watching TV and see a giant wall of butterflies in the apartment featured in the show. After six weeks, I had seen four eagles, which were more than I had seen in the last ten years!

These constant signs from the Universe had me sitting high on cloud nine, which was why I was so perplexed that I still had received no news from a book agent wanting to represent me. I had asked the Universe repeatedly for signs about publication. I couldn't figure it out, especially when I woke up one day to a flood of emails, each an automated rejection slip. I wondered what I had done "wrong" this time to attract more failure with my writing.

Frustrated because I thought I had done all the things I needed to finally launch my writing career, I wondered what I had missed. I once again reached out to my dear friend, hoping she could shed some light on the reasons my writing was not a success.

Always willing to set aside time for me, my dear friend had told me to call at my earliest convenience, which I did immediately. She answered in her usual energetic fashion. I told her that even though I had worked hard, a part of me still felt stuck. Despite all the negatives I had changed into positives and the inspirational videos I watched daily to keep my positive vibration going, nothing seemed to work.

The constant entry of affirmations in my black pleather journal had no effect either. Although I filled its pages with positive sentences, something was still blocking my most significant manifestation: publication.

I began complaining to my dear friend, just as I had done nine months earlier, and once again, she listened intently while waiting for a small opening in the conversation to let me in on a little secret. She said although I had changed immensely over the last seven years, and even more over the past nine months, there was still a part of me that was being controlled by the trauma, even though I felt I had grieved. The work I was doing helped in other ways and would continue to help me move forward in my spiritual journey, but there was still a subconscious part I refused to let go of. After a deep breath, she suggested I look deeper into the base of the grief I felt I disposed of years before and really *feel* the emotions, all of them, before letting them go once and for all!

Unable to argue against the point she was making, I hung up the phone and thought about the words I ignored for years, *I am not fully healed*. I took a deep breath and felt lucky to have her on my side. I had finally found a cause to my effect and was grateful for the people who knew me best and could open my eyes to the aspects of my life I liked to pretend didn't exist.

With a strong understanding of what had to be done, painful or not, I was still thankful for all the awareness I had achieved over the last nine months. I now knew that tackling the grief fully would help get me to the highest vibration and put me in a place of receiving. Although my vibration was higher because of my daily practice, the ups and downs frustrated me. As I considered my belief I had already grieved and there was no point revisiting it, I could see now that I had been ignoring the elephant in the room all along. I thought I could get away with the bare minimum of positive thinking and frequent affirmations without having to go back and address old issues.

Beneath the surface of the change I had created stood something hidden deeper. I couldn't let go of the one thing that had been secretly running the core of my dis-ease . . . guilt. Even though I knew where the bad habits of behavioral thoughts had stemmed from, it wasn't just the intrusiveness of the patterns I was trying to undo. It was the guilt and the poor behavior I exhibited after the accident I felt could never be undone.

As I held my head in my hands, entranced in my "aha" moment, I finally realized why my biggest manifestations were still unfulfilled: my books being picked up for publication, my dream home filled with space, and the complete peace of mind that I had struggled for years to get. I was blocking anything I might receive by ignoring the true understanding of the acceptance of what had happened to me and how I handled it.

It didn't matter how much I prayed or how many principles I tackled. My most important desires would never be fulfilled until I faced the reality that my life shattered into shards of glass, and that I reacted in a way that had destroyed what little life remained.

I had never forgiven myself for my actions before or after the accident and blindly ignored the forgiveness aspect of Louise Hay's teachings. I had been too consumed by my ego to see that the source of the anxiety was deep-rooted issues within my heart and the inability to fully forgive my own behaviors. I was too busy blaming others for my miserable life experiences. Too busy thinking that all the unwanted repercussions I experienced after the accident had been pushed onto me rather than facing the idea that my reactions had been the culprit. I was the one who had bought the idea that life was one bad thing after the other with no room for happiness, success, or anything good. So I began mentally listing all the things I was grateful for, despite the pain I had caused myself over the last seven years.

With the invisible scroll of gratitude growing with each blessing I added, I was most thankful for the changes I carried out and the level of awareness I reached with everything I had learned so far. My anxiety had diminished considerably, which made my life a lot easier.

Between Louise's affirmations and Gabrielle's "choose again method," I was now successfully able to talk myself off the ledge when intrusive thoughts surfaced. I was also more aware of others around me and that I mostly responded to circumstances in a manner that was productive, not destructive, with help from Napoleon Hill. As for *The Secret*, it had started something so amazing inside of me. I never would've gotten as far as I had without Rhonda Byrne and her team of contributors.

Although grateful for the changes I made, like a vacuum sucking up the remnants of a day's mess off the floor, I wanted no crumb left behind. I wanted to start each day off walking on a clean floor, which meant I would need to do more than just vacuum. I would need to sand, buff, and wax daily until the floor was so clean the only thing showing was the beauty it carried from the beginning, before it got walked all over. Grime.

With the guidance of my dear friend, I realized what I needed to do to finally heal from the trauma once and for all. I needed to fully free my mind, letting go of the dark spaces that filled the canvas of my life where color used to be.

After Damin died, I began living as if I had perished with him. I had created my own black hole whose darkness I allowed to control me, sucking me in and preventing me from living life to the fullest. It seemed natural to blame and punish myself for the way I had behaved both before and after he died.

The hard work I had put in over the last several years had been great, but it wasn't enough. I had released a portion of the trauma, and although that portion was significant, there were still pieces left behind. I had refused to look at the part of healing that was holding me back…myself.

I needed to revisit my most painful experiences and feel them as if I were right there all over again, only this time around I'd be armed with the right equipment to do so. As I mentally gathered all I had learned, I knew I could banish my old demons. I reflected on all the other ailments I already tackled and felt ready to complete the task successfully this time.

I was proud as I reflected on the challenges I had overcome: addiction, alcoholism, PTSD, and bulimia. I felt like an Olympic gold medalist who had competed in a series of unfortunate events and was ready to enter her last competition. The race to forgiveness would be just as easy as the others, *if* I let it be.

And now I was ready to kick the source of the habits for good, which meant forgiving myself and letting go of the guilt I carried. Now I was more aware of the concept behind our individual journey and understood everything I experienced in life was intended to shape me into the person I was supposed to be. Every heartache, every childhood problem, every adult suffering that broke me down to a tiny shred of a being was all a part of something immense that I could never understand, no matter how hard I tried.

Remembering my gold medals, I spent the next three weeks going over the years that led up to that dreadful day and everything that followed. Afterward, I could see that just when we think we're free of our past demons, they show up looking for a room to rent. We recognize the familiar face at the door and willingly let them in, not knowing that they plan to stay for good. What we don't realize is that they only stay as long as we allow them to.

I had been like a vacuum cleaner, sucking up one bad thought after another because my mind was so stuck inside my unproductive pattern of thinking. The guilt that I had placed on myself fueled me, and it only exacerbated my grief. Even though I grieved my losses, continuing on with my life, I had never let go of my guilt about not being the best girlfriend or mother. Instead,

I blamed circumstances for destroying my well-being. I could see that my stubbornness had prevented me from forgiving myself.

As painful as it was to relive the moments, the smells, the sights, and the heartaches, I felt lighter after doing so. Even though what happened in my life had brought such dysfunction, I understood it was now safe for me to live again and enjoy life.

As soon as I released the initial seed that had sprouted all my anxious thoughts, I could already feel the fresh air filling my lungs. My step was lighter and my touch warmer. There was an ease in my breath as I inhaled and exhaled, and that was something I hadn't felt for a long while.

Reexamining memories of that day made me more vulnerable to being triggered. I could feel it when I pulled back the Band-Aid to expose the wound. During the three weeks I took to reflect, my eczema had come back and seemed to spread as fast as the pandemic sweeping through our country and around the world.

I knew wounds needed time to air out and dry, and that triggers I couldn't control would be thrown at me from time to time. What I could control was how I reacted. So I began increasing my daily affirmations to help, and just as before, my red, itchy patches dried up, dissolving back into the beautiful brown skin I had always been blessed with.

I started singing new affirmations and thought patterns throughout the day, just as Louise had suggested in her book. I danced around the house and came up with catchy hits to tune out the noise of the world. Instead of falling victim to the surrounding circumstances, I did things to help, not worsen them. I turned off the news completely and stopped reading it online. I shut off the news feeds and deactivated my social media accounts.

Instead, I focused on the fact that I was just a few weeks away from being a college graduate. As I spent more time on developing closeness within my family, I was seeing a big difference in my vibration. I could feel the shift, and it was amazing. Life seemed to glow with a new light. I was thankful for the Universe and all it offered me. Years of training in anxiety and fear had prompted me to create a new forcefield around my energy, shielding me from any thoughts that didn't serve me.

At first, I was disappointed, knowing I could have changed things a long time ago by shifting my thoughts and feelings, but then I remembered what Napoleon Hill had said. Finding positivity among adversity was the only way to turn it into a stepping stone. In that moment, digging deep to find the silver lining in the years I spent in a place of darkness, a thousand bells rang loudly in my ear, as loud and clear as they had seventeen years before. The voice that had spoken to me as I drove over the bridge that day as a teen spoke to me again, telling me of the book I was destined to write.

I grabbed a piece of paper from the scrap drawer and frantically began searching for a writing utensil as I held the voice steady in my mind. Buried in the stack of baby books, I unearthed a blue Bic and wrote in large, sloppy letters as quickly as I could: "Book about healing, manifestation, and success."

As I sat on the bar stool, everything hit me, flowing in a way I had never experienced. All the suffering I put myself through had been for a higher purpose of helping others, guiding them to a better place through my own life experiences.

My purpose had always been to be a writer—that had never changed. But I wasn't supposed to write a memoir about darkness, but rather a book about coming into the light. I was supposed to share the universal secret of the Law of Attraction, just as Rhonda Byrne and others had done. Sharing my experience with this enduring law and how it healed my life would encourage others suffering around the world, so they too could find their path of healing. The book would lead millions to find and fulfill their definite true purpose so they could lead the lives of abundance and peace they deserved, even as I had.

Section Three

Alignment

About one week after my soul gained the forgiveness it needed, my mother phoned to say that she'd just had the most amazing experience with someone from our past. I immediately knew who she was talking about. I asked that she wait to share her story in person, so a few days later, I stopped by to hear all about it.

As we sat at opposite ends of her kitchen table, crucifixes hanging on the wall surrounded us. She placed her forearms on top of the wooden surface, leaned forward, and clasped her hands together. I listened as she explained how she had gone to the Blessed Sacrament Church to pray. Upon leaving to do errands, she first planned to run to the Dollar Store but had a strong urge to go to the pharmacy first.

As she stood in line waiting for her prescription, she heard a familiar voice calling her name. She turned around, knowing who it was before she even laid eyes on him. There, Kevin, the driver from the accident, sat in his wheelchair and greeted her with a friendly hello. What she told me next only brought more awareness of how powerful healing would be, and what I could attract in allowing it to happen.

As I sat on the edge of my chair, waiting to hear more, she explained he had developed a serious infection and had been about to undergo surgery when his vitals started failing . . . fast. Aware of what was going on and thinking it was the end, he told my mother the first person he thought of was my son De'Andre. Then he thought of Damin and realized the extent of the tragedy and what he had done to cause it. He understood the severity of the pain he had brought to everyone. As he felt himself slipping away, it was the thought of leaving his young child behind, the way Damin had, that allowed him to push hard and fight his way back. Not wanting to have his child grow up without a father like De'Andre, he managed to defeat death.

At the end of the conversation, he informed my mother that he prayed for De'Andre and me every single day.

As I absorbed everything she said, I experienced the same feeling of heat I'd had that day in the church with him, only this time it seemed different. My shoulders loosened, sinking further down into my body, as everything I had spent weeks going over flashed before me in an instant.

I thought of the accident, De'Andre, restorative justice, and the suffering I had inflicted on myself. I thought of the day I stood before a judge, asking for any form of punishment to pay justice to Damin because he had lost his life. As I ran through everything in my mind like a remote control clicking through various stations, something happened. For the first time in seven years, I finally felt a release because Kevin now understood his reckless behavior and how many lives he had impacted.

All his earlier apologies had felt worthless because I'd been trying to crawl through the mess of my life. Even though he did not know of the guilt I had taken on after the accident or my plummeting mental health, I now felt an indescribable moment of peace.

As I wiped the tears off my cheeks, I embraced the emotion before letting it pass. I recognized I had attracted their meeting because I had allowed my own self-inflicted wounds to heal. The Universe had moved people and circumstances to provide extra peace that I hadn't expected.

On the drive home, I prayed to Damin as I often did for spiritual support for De'Andre. I thanked him for watching over our son and told him I was doing much better and not to worry. I was thankful for the painful process I put myself through just weeks before and could feel more growth developing each day.

When I called my dear friend to tell her what took place, she got chills over what had transpired and its significant timing. She explained it was all a part of the healing journey and said she was proud of me for putting my mind and emotions in a place that allowed me to continue to heal. She insisted that reflecting on the pain had given me more than just clarity; it had given me a chance to listen. A chance to bring more peace. A chance to allow more healing.

She concluded her therapeutic pep talk by emphasizing that healing was not about forgetting, because one could never forget. The accident and Damin's death would always be there. Healing meant I was learning to deal with the reality of what had happened in a way that still allowed me to live in the most light. To live in a state that supported me to be the best for my children, helping them to flourish and not become witness to my previous anxiety.

With graduation right around the corner, and despite the global pandemic that had slowly made its way to the state of Maine, my family and I were healthy, happy, and headed in the proper direction.

As I continued to climb the ladder upward toward the vibration I most desired, my inner light encouraged me to do more self-improvement. So I took the inspired action calling me and began making more changes. I started exercising, though perfunctorily. My new motto was "on my time, at my pace." I didn't do anything that pulled me in a direction that didn't feel right.

I started listening to my mind and body, letting it tell me what it needed and what it didn't. I became more involved with dietary supplements and researched all the benefits of spices, seeds, and other natural ways to increase my nutrients. I made Tropical Turmeric Smoothies[12], Magnificent Hot Matcha Lattes[13], and doused my salads with hemp seeds and rich omega-filled oils. I cut out added sugar, still treating myself to my weakness, a Nestle Drumstick, which I loved almost even more than chips. I took my vitamins and increased my water intake to flush out toxins and waste that didn't belong. Within weeks, my hair looked shinier, and my skin was more radiant, but most importantly, I felt even healthier.

The dietary changes prompted me to research my beauty products and find "cleaner" brands. A makeup carnivore from a young age, I was a frequent user of top-name brands and designer makeup. If it was expensive, intriguing, and bold, I owned it.

After inspecting the ingredients in the products I used most, it shocked me to learn how many contained toxic substances. I had never imagined the eyeshadow in my favorite palettes were hazardous. Every time I smeared the powdery paint over my lids, all I thought about was whether I could blend it more attractively than the day before.

So I made a switch to a beauty brand that had removed over 1,800 harmful chemicals from their products. Weeding out the old and replacing it with the new, I smiled that much more when I used my clean products. As I got ready for my day, I thanked each item for its safety and thanked the Universe for providing me with the funds to purchase it.

Besides switching my makeup and diving into the world of supplements, I changed all my hair and body care products. I wanted nothing but *clean* on my skin. I loved the idea of everything natural, externally and internally, and the more changes I made, the more my family noticed and jumped on board as well.

Before I knew it, we were all drinking smoothies filled with natural nutrients. Ground flax seed, protein powder, organic fruit, and more—together we changed our diets. My family was changing, growing closer before my eyes, and it felt so good. I could see how a shift within myself had attracted a shift within my family. There were fewer arguments, less bickering, and more laughter radiating throughout the small condo. Suddenly, the walls that once felt so confining felt nurturing as the strength of our family grew. For the first time in years, I was happy in my home.

With changes happening fast around me, steadily rising to a higher vibration each day, I realized that the beneficial feelings of unity and health had always been there waiting for me to discover them. It had been my own thoughts and reactions that had taken me out of that vibration, unable to see the good that was already there.

I saw things were always good if I could rise above adversity. I also saw that if I changed my reaction to uncomfortable situations and found stepping stones among the turbulence, I would not fall into despair. The wobble was still there, but I was understanding how to keep my balance. I was steadier than ever before when taunted with challenges.

My new optimism was challenged when my tax accountant called to tell me that, because I had stayed home with the baby instead of working the previous year, I wouldn't be getting my usual child tax credit that consisted of thousands of dollars. In fact, I wouldn't be receiving anything at all because I paid no tax.

I mentally questioned if there could be a mistake. I knew my accountant was thorough, helpful, and had his shit together. His T's were always crossed, and I's perfectly dotted. He had done my taxes for many years, and I trusted him. Surely, he knew what he was talking about, but a part of me wanted him to be wrong.

The lump in my throat sat heavy as I swallowed and politely hung up the phone. I called my stepmother, who every year took part in a work program filing taxes for individuals who needed help. She confirmed that to receive tax refunds, one must work.

I couldn't hang up soon enough. I ran to the bathroom, fell to the floor, and cried, terrified of not having ample money to live on. Just as I felt the full force of a pity party coming on, I heard my teachings reminding me that my fear of not having enough money to pay my bills would only bring more of not having enough. So I lifted my head high, stood up, looked at my worried reflection in the mirror, and boldly asserted, "You have plenty. You have a constant river of money flowing to you. You will receive checks in the mail. You are blessed, and the Universe provides for you. Always."

With my chin held high as a confident reminder that I controlled the level of my vibration, I opened the door and walked out with a new attitude.

From that day forward, every time I went to the mailbox, I repeated the mantra I had spoken firmly that day in the bathroom. I acted as if I were going to pick up checks from the mail. I even skipped down the narrow pathway that led to the condo boxes with excitement, screaming out "money" with each hop. And every bill I paid, I blessed with love, just as Louise Hay said she did every time she made a payment.

A week later, my accountant called to say he had found a renter's rebate and a reimbursement for being in college, a total of $1,900. I was thrilled, delighted! I jumped for joy, nearly touching the popcorn ceiling in my excitement.

A few days after that, the House of Representatives passed the trillion-dollar stimulus check for Americans to use toward economic growth and bailouts after COVID-19 hit hard everywhere. With the $1,200 I'd receive individually, plus the additional $500 for each child, in a matter of weeks I went from being told I had no tax refund to suddenly having $4,100 in transit to my bank account!

I saw that the substantial funds hadn't been a coincidence. The Universe was showing me that, with trust, it would provide everything I needed. There wasn't anything the Universe couldn't deliver, and as long as I expected that it could and would, I had nothing to worry about.

After the blessings of unexpected money, I continued to sit contentedly on cloud nine. I was fully grasping the logic behind the Law of Attraction and felt comfortable with my progress. I was mastering new things and continued to receive signs daily, gifts from the Universe for the changes I was making.

Sometimes, I would see a cluster of signs in such a brief span, which made me think it was too easy. I found myself "double-sign seeking," wanting another sign to confirm that the one I'd just seen was real. Deep down I knew that it was, but I could feel the doubt trying to make its way through. My old belief was that things came hard, and nothing was ever easy, so I had to gently remind myself to never question the sign, but to embrace and trust in it. That all things came easily, including signs.

I told myself to relax in the enjoyment of what the Universe was providing for me because the higher the vibration I maintained, the more I would receive. So seeing signs one right after the other was a good indicator that I was headed in the right direction.

As I proceeded to float downstream, watching the scenery of signs line the sides of the metaphorical riverbank, I breathed in the spring air as the last remnants of winter faded away. I had four weeks left before I would be a college graduate. As I intended to write after graduation, I started making notes for my new book.

Whenever an idea popped into my head, I wrote it down on a scrap of paper and filed it for reference. I used the Notes app on my phone to record any thoughts I needed to share in the teaching memoir I would create. I began listening to Abraham-Hicks on YouTube when I wasn't writing papers on the linkage between biogenetics and criminal activity, and what the recidivism rate was for statistical crime. I wanted to increase my knowledge of the Universe and the Law of Attraction in any way I could, so my readers would benefit most from my writing.

Abraham-Hicks was a name I first encountered while reading *Super Attractor*. Esther Hicks and her husband Jerry were well known in the world of those who followed the laws of the Universe. Together, they traveled the world spreading their insightful messages. Esther was the speaker at their well-attended

METAMORPHOSIS

engagements. Her voice was soothing, relaxing, and comfortably hypnotic. She was a celebrity among those who believed that they co-created their lives with help from Source and alignment with their inner being.

At first, I was confused by the reference to Abraham. I had to phone my dear friend and ask how Esther Hicks operated and just who this Abraham guy was. It turned out that Abraham was Esther's Source who revealed teachings to be shared for the betterment of others. Still puzzled and intrigued by how the two interacted, I went to the Abraham-Hicks official website and clicked on, "About Abraham."

The Hicks' referred to Abraham as "a group consciousness from the nonphysical dimension," "infinite intelligence," and "the purest form of love." Abraham was Esther's Source, just like my dear friend had said, but I read further that Source was the feeling of powerful energy consisting of bliss, joy, exhilaration, love, and more. It was the energy that flowed through us, and we were all an extension of Source energy. Powerful and unseen, Source was behind the inspiration we received when in alignment with our inner being. In a YouTube video, Esther explained Source was whatever one wanted to call it, but that most referred to it as God.

Always speaking confidently and with ease, Esther relayed the wise words of Abraham in a way that seemed so effortless, even angelic, as she shared ways to increase your vibration and deal with everyday stuff that threatened to bog you down.

Together, their messages were like a massage for the brain, easing stressful thoughts as they offered guidance to those around the world who believed in their work. The dynamic duo (physical and nonphysical) were spiritual parents giving an intense surge of peace and clarity to their listeners, and I was happy to be among them.

The poignant Abraham teachings were based on twelve perceptual beliefs.[14] Not only were the beliefs enthralling, but they made sense combined with everything I had learned. Abraham-

Hicks soon became a part of my daily routine. Everything they said made complete sense, as if they were speaking directly to me. I flagged their YouTube videos—nearly a hundred of them—thumbs up, and every time I replayed one, I gained new insight.

I learned that I was a magnificent human with an inner being, and that there wasn't anything I couldn't do or have. That alignment with my inner being would always be the direct route to everything I desired. And that my inner being was my nonphysical self or soul.

The connection with our inner being allows us to draw closer to our passions, dreams, and true calling. It allows intuitive messages of synchronicity to further expand our awareness and to exist in a world we want to create. Most importantly, our inner being allows us to do anything by providing us with vast clarity through the promotion of healing, spiritual development, and internal insight to reveal our true persona.

According to Abraham-Hicks, when connected to our inner being through high energy vibrations, which is the *only* way to connect, the Law of Attraction will extract and magnify those energies bringing forth wondrous manifestations from whatever was placed inside the "vortex," a never-ending river collecting our dreams and desires as we swim along thought by thought. That's why being conscious of what we want is so crucial.

Through the connection with our inner being, we would gain clarity that enables us to hear the inspiration Source communicating to help us attain our desires. The inspiration obtained through clarity would reveal ways to manifest the specific desires placed into the vortex: love, health, success. Eventually, the Universe would bring these desires into physical form through the Law of Attraction.

To help their followers easily understand the quickest route to gain access to what was placed in the vortex, Abraham-Hicks created an easy five-step process.

Step one was simply asking. A straightforward request for what was wanted formed through "contrasted experiences." The beautiful part about step one was that we were constantly doing it without even noticing. Everything that happened daily that opposed feeling good helped us to be aware of what would feel better instead.

Step two consisted of knowing that once a desire was asked for, it was given. Always. As soon as a "rocket of desire"[15] was launched, Source answered every time.

Step three was about choosing thoughts intentionally, so your thoughts and feelings matched vibrationally with what was being asked.

Step four had to do with receiving, opening up to the idea that there was good energy all around and that things were always getting better. And that through alignment with your inner being, you would place yourself in what Abraham-Hicks referred to as "receptive mode," which was necessary to receive what was being asked.

Finally, step five was about not being so tough on yourself when you wind up back at step one, because there would always be another step one. The work was never done so the steps would be repeated. New desires would be sought daily, and it was our job to see that when faced with "contrasted experiences."

As I acknowledged the process of all five steps, I loved how similar they were to the other teachings I had studied. That anything I wanted was mine if I asked. That circumstances would pop up, but how I reacted, launching new rockets of desire, would be the key to success. Complete control was mine *if* I could see it.

Because of all I was learning from Esther and her team of "infinite intelligence," I was feeling more in tune with my inner being every day.

I felt new. Lighter. More aware of the people around me and vibes they were putting out, which helped determine who I was in sync with. I discovered that my vibrational radar was helping me sense where to shine the light beaming from my body on those who needed it most. I also found that my schoolwork and term papers were getting completed in record time, and I accomplished all my household tasks with ease.

With each passing day rising higher in vibration, I started seeing recurring numbers of *10, 11,* and *22,* in addition to the universal signs I had already observed. Each day, the volume of the digits increased, as well as their variety.

I first noticed their presence on the stove clock, representing minutes: *5:10, 3:11, 10:22*; soon, the double digits doubled and tripled. I began catching the time frequently falling on *10:10, 11:11, 1:11,* and *2:22*. I knew the sequence of the numbers was no coincidence, and when I looked up their meaning, it elated me by what I found.

After some Internet research, I gravitated toward a website called The Secret of The Tarot, and discovered that guardian angels communicated with us through numerical signs called "angel numbers."

Number *10* was a representation of new beginnings and a sign that we are not alone. That as spiritual and physical beings, we have access to divine energies to assist us at any given time.

As I perused the site, I remembered reading something similar in *Super Attractor*. Gabrielle had talked about spirit guides and how being open to the idea of them and their help would increase the connection with one's inner being. It would also bring ease and clarity when one felt confused. The help you could ask your guides for was endless; they were there to help raise us to the highest place of positive intentions. . . always!

The rest of the description of angel number *10* continued to amaze me. It was also a sign to trust in the guardians around us to receive the inspirations or solutions they were trying to get across to us. Number *10* was a forceful reminder that the support being offered from unseen assistance was to help raise our vibration to come into alignment with Source.

METAMORPHOSIS

When the number was duplicated, *1010*, it was a supportive sign to stay on track, maintain a positive mindset, and know that the guides were there to love and encourage us.

I joyfully perused his site to discover the meaning of the rest of my angel numbers.

11: Considered a master number, *11* signified communication from angels seeking to inspire you to further develop your abilities to better the existence of humanity. Sitting at a high vibration, it also stood for leadership and a positive outlook.

111: Spiritual awakening, co-creating realities, new beginnings, and career changes, this number spoke of revealing your gifts, following what makes you passionate, and finding and expressing your unique abilities. Remaining true to who you are, *111* further signified gratitude for *all* things. And finally, to celebrate every area of wellness in your life to attract more.

1111: This number advised you of your ability to connect with ascended masters in the angelic realm and with the energy coming from Source. Like *11*, the number quadrupled represented new beginnings and a transformation that would offer new opportunities for wisdom. It was also a chance to increase self-esteem and discover areas of truth about yourself that align you with your thoughts and actions. *1111* was a symbol to have faith and a reminder that help was all around to support you on your journey.

22: Another master number guiding you to move forward in harmony and faith as you created your inner desires. Powerful in its symbolism, it was a message that you were close to getting spiritual wisdom that was meant to be shared with the world. You were also close to the highest form of alignment, and you should trust in the guides who were leading you there.

222: A firm reminder to rebalance, banishing negative thoughts of fear that didn't serve you. You should persist and remain positive with a productive attitude. Letting you know you were on the right path to achieve your dreams, it also meant to be aware of decisions, and that you were meant to serve everyone you encountered and bring them greater good.

After I'd analyzed the meaning of each number, my sightings skyrocketed. While driving, I noticed license plates that proclaimed *222* or *1111*. When I watched TV or checked the time on my phone or stove, I couldn't escape the numbers, nor did I want to.

It didn't matter what TV movie or series I watched. When C.J. and I binge-watched *Dexter,* the numbers would appear as crime scene evidence markers or clocks frozen in time. Sometimes it was a calendar with the date *11* circled in red or a number on the back of a game jersey. No matter what I watched, the numbers appeared to me. . . always.

Or I'd be in deep thought about something placed inside of my vortex as I walked into the kitchen to get a drink, and *11:11, 1:11,* or *2:22* would stare right at me. Even if I were thinking a thought that didn't serve me, I would see *10:10* or another number in my line of vision. In that moment of negative thought, the numbers acted as a deterrent, pulling me away and getting my thinking back on track.

Regardless of what I was doing, the numbers were everywhere. So much so that I kept track for one week to calculate the number phenomenon consuming me.

I loaded all angel numbers into an Excel spreadsheet, and for seven days, I took a tally, never missing a number. By the end of the week, it dumbfounded me by how often they appeared. In a single week, I had seen the number *10* twenty-one times and *1010* eleven times. Coming in strong at fifty-four, the number *11* had popped up the most, followed by *111*, fourteen times.

Another high-vibrational number, *1111,* came into sight four times and *222* showed its presence six times. In total, I had received one hundred and ten numerical signs from my guides in seven days. The best part was that the messages were making their way to me after I allowed the gates to open, letting my heart, mind, and soul adjust to the vibrational level I needed to receive more.

I took my documented research to heart and knew that fully healing had allowed me to seek improved opportunities for alignment, opening doors that would have remained closed if I hadn't taken the time to reflect on what was holding me back. Grateful for all the help I was receiving from my spirit guides, I carried on full force toward my definite major purpose.

When the first week of May arrived, I felt new, just like the flowers blooming. I accomplished one of the largest goals I had set, graduating magna cum laude with an associate science degree in criminology and criminal justice.

After six years of schooling on and off, I finally had a diploma to call my own. The hard work had paid off and it felt amazing. Amazing that I had persevered. Amazing that I had a partner who worked hard and allowed me to stay at home and complete my education. Amazing that I never gave up, even though at times I'd wanted to.

Sailing smoothly on the coattails of my long overdue accomplishment, I was excited to get writing. Three days into the book I was born to write, I sat there staring blankly at the computer. It wasn't writer's block; rather, I was overwhelmed by the amount of work I had ahead of me. I had already written so many papers, as well as three unpublished books, but I was uncertain how I would serve the world with new and old concepts about manifestation and healing. I wanted every word to be perfect, insightful, and meaningful, and the idea of falling short was nerve-racking.

Unable to take off strong, I was lost and trying to find my way back. Writing was my passion. My gift. My purpose. Something I never had felt despondent about. As I sat at the kitchen table with still fingers and a quiet keyboard, I questioned the profound inspiration I'd recently gathered and doubted my ability to deliver it.

As I shut down the computer, sulking amid my failure to write that day, the image of Gina Self popped into my head. It had been months since I'd last talked to her, and even though I had gone against her suggestions, I was now ready to follow her advice. With my tail between my legs, I pulled up her scheduling link and took the first available appointment three weeks away. I also texted her and asked if she could put me on her cancellation list. In less than twenty minutes, I had an affirmative reply.

I knew the sooner I talked to her, the better, so I sent my request out to the Universe and trusted that something would open up sooner. The next day, she asked if I could do a phone session the following afternoon. I was thrilled and knew I made the right decision in reaching out to her and to the Universe.

That night, I couldn't fall asleep. Like a child waiting for Christmas Day to come, I was anxious and excited and wondering what I would find. As I tossed and turned, I created a mental list of things I wanted to ask her. Without a doubt, I knew I wanted to know why I was seeing all the numbers. I wanted to know why I felt sudden rushes of old anxieties at times. And I wanted to know if my spirit guide had a name and if my intuition was correct about the direction of the new book.

The next morning, I wrote all my questions neatly on the back of my original manuscript. I went over which ones I would ask first, categorizing them according to importance, and made a small list of extras in case there was enough time to go over them.

I paced back and forth for most of the day and watched the digital clock change on the stove . . . slowly. Time seemed to slow down that afternoon. The only thing that kept me relaxed enough to enjoy the idea that I would soon talk to Gina was watching my angel numbers pop up throughout the day.

After building a lengthy bridge of anticipation, about fifteen minutes before the call, I prepped the baby for contentment. I made sure she was full and fed, and put on her favorite movie, *Angry Birds 2*. I told De'Andre I had an important phone call and passed him his snack early . . . Cliff bar and a juice box. The choice of snack was just enough to keep him satisfied for my thirty minutes of peace. A preteen, naturally he was eating me out of house and home!

With sweaty palms, I watched the minutes drag by. Then, at 3:04, Gina called. Immediately, any reservations I had about what she would say to me evaporated. Her warm voice felt kind and assuring.

We briefly caught up, and I told her how I had failed to take her advice about rewriting the book. I told her about the romance novel and how that too had gone unrepresented. Then I said I had finally come to terms with the book I was destined to write and told her all about it.

Without hesitation, she said that was exactly what I was supposed to do. That the book I was supposed to write was meant to be uplifting and would help many people. That I was a star seed. A light worker. And that my purpose on earth was to help the world with my gift . . . writing. Gina said she saw many books written in me. She also saw me speaking at seminars, which was what a psychic had told my mother when I was just sixteen years old.

She then explained that the recent bout of anxiety I had experienced was due to how quickly things were changing for me. She stated I was powerful, and I needed to make sure my thoughts were productive. She said that I would have slipups occasionally, but that I needed to let go of the old habits that were trying to sneak back in and restrict me.

Although I needed to be wise about what thoughts I invited into my life, I also had to know I was human, and it was okay to think "weird" things from time to time. A medical intuitive, Gina reassured me I was going to be around for a long, long time. But she did kindly remind me I also needed to know that we all have the power to create problems in our body, which made complete sense after reading Louise's book.

I was feeling more at ease and decided it was time to ask her about the numbers and why I was seeing them so frequently. Just as the angel numbers website had taught me, Gina said the numbers were a way of communication from my guides. She told me I had guides all around me. At all times.

One in particular, a male shaman from so long ago she didn't even know how to pronounce the name she was hearing, was the one helping me write. After a pause, she explained he was telling her he came to me when I was most relaxed. She said to take note as to where, when, and what position I was in when I felt I was flowing most with my words. And in that moment, to know that he was with me.

I felt chills and goosebumps take over my body, and I knew just what she was talking about. I knew where I'd sat, how I'd sat, and the time of day that had placed me in a sort of trance, processing words faster than I could type. I had always felt that something stronger, something out of my realm, was moving me to write. It felt like a force was taking over and bringing me to a place I never could have gotten to on my own. It felt magical, and I was well aware of the difference when it was absent.

Moving on, referring back to numbers and their meanings, she suggested I would start seeing the number four in addition to the elevens and twos she saw all around me. The number four signified a high vibration and signified my connection to a group of children whose intention was focused on fixing the world, and that I would one day help those children and guide their parents in ways that would facilitate their goal.

I absorbed all she said, especially when she told me I had a time limit and was not supposed to take years to write the book, as it then wouldn't reach the people who needed it. I had felt the same thing, which often added pressure to the idea of writing it correctly and in a timely manner. I felt I could most likely finish the book in four months, and Gina agreed.

Before hanging up, I graciously thanked her and said I'd be in touch when the book was completed. The next day, I thought constantly about our conversation. Everything she said made sense. Everything she explained through her intuitive gift seemed to validate all that I had sensed on my own. It gave me peace and insight that I couldn't achieve on my own. Gina had opened a door for me, and I was beyond grateful.

That evening prepping dinner and thinking of Gina and her wonderful self, I glanced over to the clock on the stove to estimate when everything would be ready. I stopped in my tracks when I saw the time: 4:44. Just as she had explained, fours had been added to the list of numbers that were being communicated to me.

The following morning, the number 44 was everywhere. The day after that, even more so. Fueled with the support from Gina and the invisible guides around me, I opened my computer and began to write with limber fingers, stretching and hitting the keys faster than Bruce Lee striking his opponent. I wrote smoothly and effortlessly.

As I typed like an expert, the words that needed to get across to help others came out quicker than I could keep up. I was getting so much work done, and in just a few hours' time. I just kept writing with no intention of stopping. I had called out to my spirit guide by the name I had given him, Shaman, and asked for his guidance before I wrote and thanked him generously when I was finished for the day.

Flowing naturally with the writing current that had captivated me, I enjoyed the feeling of accomplishment and the confidence of the momentum. Some days, I had to be torn away from the computer. The fact that I was weeks away from molding the perfect manuscript to help others I had never met, just like the mentors who helped me, was humbling. Even when I wasn't working on the computer, I was writing in my head, but I still took breaks to be with my family.

One day, the four of us—C.J., the kids, and I—went for a walk together. We posed in the shadowed shade of an old oak tree for C.J. to take a few pictures of us with the camera on his new iPhone 11. Later that evening, we went back to review the snapshots together, and the photos were unlike anything I had ever seen before.

Perfectly placed in the direction of my son stood ten large beams, broken into different segments and separated by various colors. Each segment was colored differently from the segment next to it. Like an alternating strobe light shining over him, one beam's segment started with yellow, then orange and purple before ending with green.

The next beam was blue, yellow, orange, and then purple, trailing off to green. The remaining eight were all different, and the closest and largest beam that sat between my son and me was green, orange, purple, yellow, and what seemed to blend into a brilliant orange again.

I knew that the sporadically segmented, rainbow beams were our guides surrounding us. I was enthralled with the captured image of spirit light. I immediately sent the picture to my mother and my dear friend, who both saw the same thing I'd seen, guardians and guides walking with us, showering us with protective light. I also sent the image to Gina Self, who confirmed our findings. The captured images of colored light were a firm reminder that some invisible things can, under certain circumstances, become visible.

It felt amazing to have the visual encounter, and again exactly when I needed it most. I treasured the connection I was carrying with my guides and invited them into my day every morning when I prayed.

As the weeks went on, the more I wrote, the more signs I got. I knew it was my guides telling me to keep up the good work or guiding me to hear something I needed. They sometimes woke me in the middle of the night to tell me things to write about. I was amazed.

I was even more amazed when I awoke one early morning with a specific song lyric playing in my head letting me know that anything I wanted, I could have and then checking the time to reveal it was *4:11* a.m. Or, waking up at *4:44* a.m. with a precise insight about something to add to the book.

The messages that they were sending me were strong and continuous, never stopping. Even in my sleep. Dreaming *1111* on elevators or seeing *222* as I drifted off, everywhere I went, even REM sleep, there were signs.

During my waking hours, there were giant signs, and often right in front of my face. Confirmation numbers in emails reading *111* or emails delivered at *2:22* were frequent occurrences. Or walking down the street with my children and noticing a vanity plate reading *"11-Elevn"* while I was thinking about my vortex.

Every time I jumped into my Jeep, I saw more and more license plates reading *1010, 111, 222,* and *44*, alone or in combination with other numbers. Sometimes, I would see the same car skirting around town with only *222* on it.

What was even cooler is I would drive down the road and feel a gentle hand turning my head to look over. When I did, I'd see my numbers again, *10, 11, 22,* and *44* on the sides of random houses scattered throughout the roads I was traveling on. Even better, one time while driving southbound on the interstate to see my family, I heard a voice telling me to look over, and I saw an eagle perched in a tree. He was big, beautiful, and bold as he watched me zoom past him.

The signs in the waking hours didn't stop there. They kept coming in all forms. The digital clock on the stove and my cell phone would reveal a number every hour: *10, 11, 22, 44* in minute form and in constant variations with the hour. Sometimes, I would see all four in a single hour. That was in addition to seeing the heavy hitters like, *10:10, 11:11, 1:11, 2:22* and *4:44*, all appearing at times I needed them to, just as they always had.

Sometimes I would catch the minute just before, but then would watch it change to the angel number. It always made me feel as if I were just on the cusp of something, and that if I were patient long enough and put in the effort, I would uncover something magical.

Sometimes I would catch the number after, but finding positivity in the missed digit, I could see that it was a sign to perhaps slow down or re-orchestrate what I was thinking at that moment.

When I added purple flowers to my list of significant signs to be noticed after a disagreement with my mother on Mother's Day, I started seeing them everywhere. On Mother's Day, my aunt hand-delivered a gorgeous flower bouquet from my mother, whose petals looked like delicate bells dangling from their stem. I was upset because I had not wanted to bring unnecessary items into the house during the pandemic. After switching my vibration from fearing the flowers to loving them, I felt it was appropriate to use them as another beautiful sign from the Universe, representing the love and appreciation I had for my mother.

Suddenly, little purple flowers were spreading their radiant color along my walkway for the first time in the eleven years I had lived there. There were purple flowers in the shows I watched, purple flowers in the fields as I drove by, and purple flowers and butterflies on the special card I received from a friend to whom I had sent a copy of Louise Hay's *You Can Heal Your Life*.

Wherever I looked, signs followed me like a trail of breadcrumbs left by my spirit guides in order to lead me home. Home to a place that had always been waiting for me. Home to living a life I was meant to live, filled with an abundance of success and well-being in a place of absolute vibrational alignment.

My guides woke me up whenever I drifted over the rumble strip of my old patterns, and I could feel their helpful presence with me constantly. Eleven months into the journey, I was at the highest vibration I had ever reached. I knew it was only a matter of time before I fulfilled my greatest dream... publication!

Envisioning life as I wanted and the new manifestations I would attract in achieving my definite major purpose, I thought of the foundation I would create, Care for Kids, with some finances from the book. I thought of the people I would employ, veterans and victims of domestic violence, or perhaps recently paroled individuals who had committed low-level crimes. Taking what I had learned in criminology, recidivism rates could often be lowered if people knew they had a chance to survive after making their mistakes, a chance at living productively again and not being judged for their past.

In college, I had learned about an organic bread company where one out of three employees have criminal backgrounds.

Dave Dahl spent fifteen years in prison. When it came time to find work, which is hard for parolees, his brother offered him a job at the family bakery. Dave took his job seriously and worked diligently on creating a new, organic, non-GMO bread formula. After discovering the perfect recipe and debuting Dave's Killer Bread at the Portland Farmers Market in 2005, the rest was history. According to their website, Dave's Killer Bread is the number one organic bread brand in America.

Seeing how Dave Dahl gave people a chance to have new beginnings by opening doors that usually remained closed, especially for parolees, I knew that was what I wanted to do. In the grand scheme of things, I just wanted to help other people who felt stuck through the dreams I manifested after getting myself unstuck.

I loved getting lost in positive thought because when I did, everything felt almost close enough to touch. I wanted so badly to hold the manifestation in my hands and knew that soon I would. However, I noticed that as the days progressed into summer; I slightly slipped every time I felt that I got a bit closer.

I worried about falling into old habits and wondering if they would come back and bite me in the ass. It was strange because I was spending so much of my day deliberately creating, only to have some stupid thought of how I used to be creep in and interfere.

I knew the Universe was beautiful and bountiful, so I understood that anything I desired in my heart would come to fruition. I also knew that once I had manifested the definite major purpose I sought to achieve, there would be no turning back, and that was scary. Again, I found myself trying to figure things out before they happened, thinking that if I did, I could stop anything looking to derail me.

I had read about the man in Louise's book, *You Can Heal Your Life*, who had won $500 on a lottery ticket. He couldn't believe that *he* had won, and almost felt he didn't deserve the money. One week later, the man fell and broke his leg; his medical expenses came to $500.

Three weeks before my thirty-fifth birthday, I wavered in thought, fearing I'd become the man with the broken leg, losing new gains to old habits. I was lost in a "mixed bag" of thoughts, as Abraham-Hicks described it. My "sloppy" thoughts, up one minute and down another, a mixed bag of experiences would be the outcome of my fluctuating, emotional rollercoaster.

I understood the importance of letting go and floating up to the surface. But bobbing around comfortably felt much more pleasing than the unpleasant hiccups that surfaced here and there. If I were doing my work correctly, finding positivity among the involuntary convulsions would act as leverage, peeling me away from the idea that I *could* be the man with the broken leg.

As I recentered myself the best I could to find a solution to my troublesome thoughts, I relaxed in the presence of my comforting beliefs. I remembered that once I resolved the thoughts derailing me, I would get back into the "path of least resistance" according to Abraham-Hicks, and back into realignment.

My yearning for realignment was strong. I could feel myself craving it as I ping-ponged between productive and unproductive thoughts, so I asked my guides and angels for help. I revisited whatever signs I had received that day or the day before to help get me back on track as well. I was grateful for the constant communications with my guides and angels and recognized that when I called out to them, I instantly felt stronger. I also saw more signs.

Here and there, little things popped up throughout my day to remind me where I wanted to be, who I was, and how to regain my rhythm. Then, a few days after gaining momentum with my realignment, the Universe sent me a bold sign to show how supported I was in my journey.

One rainy day, with sounds of distant thunder lingering in the background, the sun was playing peek-a-boo with a fading storm. Intrigued by the clouds and the colors of the sky mixing, C.J. went out to see if the storm would make a second round. When he waved for me to come join him after stepping twenty feet away from our door, I threw on my Adidas slides and ran outside to see what he had found.

He was smiling from ear to ear and told me to turn around. With bulging eyes and an open mouth, I witnessed the largest, most beautiful double rainbow I had ever seen! We stood there in awe, transfixed by the brilliant beauty and magic of Mother Nature. It was too large to fit in the camera's frame, so I took a video and sent it to my dear friend.

She too, was amazed at the beauty of the rare double rainbow. For the rest of the evening, the rainbow was all I could think about. The idea that the Universe had delivered this magnificent sign at precisely the time I needed it was beyond satisfaction.

The double dose of arched colors symbolized the Universe was working things out to my benefit. It also meant that magical paths were forming for me to walk down. As I sat on the couch, still mesmerized by the image I had seen, I silently told myself that this was it. Things were happening all around me, enabling me to achieve the success I desired to help my family and others in the world.

I knew that trying to figure out what the Universe was doing and when was not my job, and how it was doing it was completely insignificant and irrelevant to the work I had to do. What *was* my job was to trust in the timing of the things I wanted to manifest and know that they would come when they were supposed to.

The next day I woke up feeling different. And the day after that, and the day after that. I knew that one pot of gold led to another. I realigned myself even more with my inner being, and the results were amazing.

Idea after idea came, and constantly. I was receiving new inspiration daily with writing and other things in my life. It was like a constant flow of energy vibrating through me, linking all the dots together. Every time my inner being revealed something for inspiration, I would look up and see one of my angel numbers on the TV or the clock. The drive toward complete alignment was intoxicating. I would find myself in tears during moments of discovery, feeling so strongly about what was being translated through the inspiration I was receiving.

So, when my thirty-fifth birthday came a couple weeks later, and I had allowed something to stay on my mind longer than it should have, I promised myself I would finish the book in the next two months and focus on continued alignment. Reeling in all that was promising and releasing anything that wasn't serving me, I trusted that in doing so, I would finally close the gap between myself and my ultimate manifestation . . . publication.

That morning, all my family called to wish me a happy birthday. When my stepmother and father called, I felt a sudden urge to walk up the hill as we were speaking. So I connected my headphones, plopped the baby in the stroller, and followed De'Andre, who was already climbing the hill on his bike.

As I huffed and puffed a bit, pushing my toddler up the slight incline, I explained that the independent journey I had started a year ago would continue in full force. I told them this year would be better than the last and that I sensed we would soon move into a big, beautiful house.

I admitted my slipups but stressed that overall, I had changed much for the better, and they agreed. I said today would not only mark a celebration of my birth but also the day that represented an even newer journey that would bring greater opportunities and fresh beginnings for my family. I rambled on, telling them I would become even more passionate about what I wanted to achieve and more compassionate with the feelings of others.

As I approached my turnaround point at the top of the street, a four-foot rock wall dividing two driveways, I felt a gentle nudge to look down at the small patch of purple flowers growing beneath the bottom layer of rocks, and that was when I saw it. I tried not to react to scare the baby, my family on the phone, or the nearby neighbors, but sitting peacefully, basking in the rays of the sun, was a huge snake.

I stared at it just long enough to see the different colored stripes racing vertically down its slinky back. Then I quickly turned the stroller around, resisting an urge to scream, and briskly walked away. In the almost eleven years I had lived on the street, I had never seen a snake. Ever. I had goosebumps; for most of my life, I had feared and despised snakes.

As I walked away, I was thinking it had to be a sign of something more, something to do with all the amazing changes I'd been talking about. When I got off the phone with my dad, I immediately texted my dear friend, as I vaguely remembered her mentioning that seeing a snake was a good sign. I was terrified of snakes as a child, and also connected them with the fall of Adam and Eve, so it was hard for me to realize they might have a spiritual significance.

One day, in conversation with my dear friend about the frequent snake dreams I'd been having, she had shared that snakes were connected to primal energy and represented healing and transformational life changes. She further pointed out that the snake was an offering of guidance through physical, emotional, and spiritual life changes.

I realized that what I had seen was intended as a sign from my guides to let me know that through all the changes coming, in all aspects of life, they would be there by my side the whole way. The snake sighting had been a gift of support for all the hard work I had done in the past year. A gift to let me know I was on the correct path.

Four weeks later, I woke up one morning in the midst of remembering how, a year earlier, a few weeks after I started my spiritual journey, I had seen a baby snake. I was celebrating my daughter's first birthday at her aunt's spacious home. I walked around the backyard admiring the beautiful garden they had built, filled with raised beds growing everything you would ever want. I remembered thinking that one day, we would have something similar. I imagined C.J. building it himself, and the kids and me hauling organic soil from a massive compost mound in our yard.

As I watched my daughter's aunt water her growing greens and plump tomatoes, I noticed something short, black, and covered in stripes near the side of the fence. I stepped closer to get a better look, let out a small shriek, and yelled, "Snake!" She turned around and stomped her petite feet in her rain boots, hoping to scare him off. Meanwhile, I ran back up to the family deck to shake off the unexpected sighting. It had been years since I'd seen a snake, and I wasn't pleased to see this one.

I sat down on a deck chair and tried to focus my mind somewhere other than the baby snake I had encountered. I was glad it hadn't been any bigger, but wondered how I'd even noticed the small creature coiled up against the dark fence. He was nearly buried in the loose dirt that rested against the wooden posts. The very sight of him was perplexing, but I shook it off and never thought of it again until I woke up that morning a year later thinking about him.

As I lay in the comfort of my bed, hair messy and morning breath begging to be brushed fresh, I thought of the little snake I had seen that sunny July afternoon. I then thought of the enormous snake I had been frightened by just weeks earlier resting against the rock wall and realized that both snake sightings had been a gift from Shaman. By gathering the information my dear friend had shared with me about the spiritual meaning of the snake, it was clearer to me than ever. The baby snake had marked the beginning of my spiritual journey, small and eager to grow. The larger snake represented how much growth I had made in a year's time.

I shot out of bed and started dancing. I loved how my thoughts were coming together and the revelations I was able to configure that morning. It was exhilarating.

Later that morning, I took the kids and my son's friend on a walk up to an abandoned parking lot at the top of the street. I huffed and puffed as I pushed the stroller up the incline, just as I had that day on the phone with my stepmom and dad. My eyes focused on my surroundings: the beautiful houses that lined the street, the green grass growing strong, and the summer flowers radiant in their bloom. I thought about Shaman and about how, in that moment, as I walked up my street taking in all the sights, my spirit guides and guardian angels were right there walking along with me.

It was a beautiful feeling. I smiled and called out, "Thank you. I love you guys!" as I sensed their presence all around me. Just as I reached the rock wall where I had seen the snake a month earlier, I heard a voice speak to me. It was the same voice that had spoken to me that day riding over the bridge decades ago, telling me my purpose, and the same voice that instructed me what I was supposed to write about just months earlier.

The voice told me to not be afraid but, when I approached the rock wall, to look down at the small Hosta next to the purple flowers. I knew there would be another gift waiting for me. As my feet moved slowly up the incline, I questioned my sanity. Did I actually hear what I thought I heard? I could see the baby Hosta in view as my sandals crept closer, and coiled up tightly underneath the gentle shade of the Hosta was the snake. I called out, not in fear this time, but because what I'd heard really existed!

The boys scooted over to see what all the excitement was about. I told them there was a snake sleeping under the plant and that they could look but not disturb him. I knew it was the same snake from before, and the instant connection that vibrated through my body when I saw his stripes was the only confirmation I needed.

For the rest of the day, I couldn't stop thinking about the snake. I was so grateful for the second sighting of him a month later, as I had walked by that same place a dozen times since the first encounter and not seen him again. I loved how that morning I had reevaluated the meaning of snakes and how I felt about them, and then hours later, I saw him again. It was one more confirmation that what was happening to me was real. That I hadn't gone crazy, hearing voices in my head. Communication with the nonphysical help surrounding me was always possible.

A couple of weeks after my rendezvous with my slithery friend, C.J. and I were headed out to run a couple of errands before dinner. It was late afternoon, and the roofers had gone home for the day, which made it easier to leave. The forty-eight-unit condo complex we lived in was getting a new roof, and lucky for us, they had started on our side first.

Tenants were told to be careful while the work was being done. Additionally, we were told to park our vehicles away from the building so they would be protected from debris. This meant that our cars faced the new mini Wrigley baseball field and playground built for the town's youth. This field was a big deal and located right in our backyard. The colorful play structure was mostly used by baseball players, but occasionally by other locals as well.

C.J., De'Andre, Amaya, and I would go up to the field and park all the time when no one else was there. With a soccer ball and football in tow, we'd run drills and test our ball-kicking skills. It was nice to have a big athletic space nearby to work off our energy.

The summer sun made its presence known as C.J. and I walked across the parking lot and climbed into the Jeep. While we were deciding which errand to do first, I noticed a large van parked up at the field and a young child running over alone to the slides. I then felt a gentle nudge come from under my chin, lifting my head up and back over to the van. It was Kevin, the driver from the accident, who had come to spend some time with his son at the park.

A part of me couldn't believe that he was in my backyard; that at the same time I was piling into my car, he was piling out of his. But the other part of me, the aware part, knew the sighting of him was no mistake. The meeting had been lined up perfectly by the Universe.

Just a few months earlier, he had offered a small piece to the puzzle I had waited years to finish. Though he never held the key to my healing—only I could provide that—knowing how he felt now about the accident and the fact that he had thought of my son on his deathbed had softened my anger.

I whispered to C.J., "Oh, my gosh, that's Kevin, the driver from the accident."

My first instinct was to go up there to thank him for what he shared with my mother. I still remembered the expression on De'Andre's face when I told him what Kevin said to his grandmother at the pharmacy. I could see his shoulders loosen as if he had just released a load he had been carrying for many years.

A few months after the accident, my mother had taken De'Andre to McDonald's and had run into Kevin. De'Andre just stared at him while Kevin asked him random questions to ease the uncomfortable feeling that surrounded them. The exchange of words only lasted a minute or two, but one thing De'Andre remembered, even at five years old, was that Kevin did not say he was sorry.

Years after the run-in at McDonald's, after he had grieved the loss of his father, there was still a part of him that remembered everything and felt accountability was missing. Kevin sharing what he had that day with my mother was exactly what De'Andre needed to hear. Damin had been a father, a partner, a son, a brother, a nephew, and a friend, and to De'Andre, he was everything. He needed to know that the person who took his father from him understood what he had done.

I hesitated for a moment and then glanced over at his son climbing the limbs of the structure like Tarzan. I looked back toward Kevin as he rode in closer and wondered how I would say what I wanted to say? I wondered what he would say back?

I was scared. Nervous. What if I walked up there and regretted getting out of the car? What if I got up there and I became angry and ran off upset in front of his son? But then I wondered, what if I regretted not getting out of the car? What if I drove away and never got the chance to thank him for saying what he had? A piece of De'Andre had healed that day. It was something that no one else could offer him besides Kevin, and as a mother, I had to be thankful for that.

"I'm going up there," I said as I opened the door, letting in the warm August air. I swung my legs out of the car and onto the pavement. My knees wobbled, but my feet stood their ground. A deep breath filled my lungs as I began my journey up the hill. The sound of soft grass whistled under my Nikes with every step I took. I repeated their slogan, "Just Do it," over and over as I watched the distance between us shorten. Though I still felt nervous, I remembered that my spirit guides and angels were with me. Recognition of their presence washed over me like a gentle shower, giving me the strength to continue.

He came around the corner of the bleachers, and that's when I spoke. Not wanting to frighten his son, I quietly called out to him. Kevin stopped his chair and acknowledged me with a friendly nod and a pleasant hello. He introduced me to his son, telling him exactly who I was, De'Andre's mom. His son was polite and said hello as he teetered off the edge of the platform, hanging on tightly to the metal bars above his head.

My heart pounded as I searched for the right words to say, but before I could even finish the sentence, my eyes welled up with tears. My voice trembled as I told him it had been what De'Andre and I both needed to hear after all these years, accountability.

He looked over to the side of his right shoulder and then began crying. He spoke briefly, and together we cried, just as we had that day in the church years earlier. I finally collected myself and ran back to the car. It felt like years of pain slipping away, the knowledge that ownership was finally there.

When someone you love loses their life by the actions of another, you want the recognition of ownership to be there. The accountability offered a small amount of comfort for me, and for him, perhaps, a means of atonement.

Our interaction that day was short but impressionable. I walked away that afternoon even more aware of how powerful the Universe was. I saw how the Universe worked and knew that forgiving myself had, once again, brought more closure. I saw how every second of my day, and his, had lined us up perfectly for us to have a meaningful exchange of words. Nothing was coincidental, nor would it ever be. . . .

Appreciative for the growth I was experiencing and the signs I was receiving, I knew more than ever that everything I wanted was only an arm's length away. So I lived with the feeling that I had already received it, knowing it would attract it that much more quickly.

A few weeks later, I finished the book. And if you're reading these words now, then it is true. All of it. Every. Single. Last. Word. Is true. The Law of Attraction, self-healing, manifestation—all of it exists, and I am living proof that positive thoughts attract more things to be positive about. Living proof that you can be stuck in the worst pile of crap, just as I was, and come up smelling like roses. Living proof that even the wildest ideas and aspirations in life can come true.

I'm an ordinary girl from a small town in Maine, and I can tell you that if you want something bad enough, you can make it happen. Using the tools of the different mentors I attracted, who taught me everything I needed to know, I created the perfect formula that led me to success, personal achievement, healing, and peace of mind. Of course, sometimes it felt like I was pushing an elephant uphill, but the truth is, there are valuable lessons to be learned in our failures and struggles.

What I can also say now is I'm grateful for my life being as hard as it was in the past. Cliché, but if it hadn't been for the bad parts I created, I never would have gotten to where I am today. Where I am, *now*. You need a little, or even a lot of darkness now and then to know where to shine the light. It's all a part of the human experience, how we "rise above."

The things in life that challenge us, breaking us down to a lower level of vibration, eventually get us to where we're supposed to be. If one thing had changed, we wouldn't be who we are. We wouldn't be what we experienced, building us to a place of determination and perseverance.

I hated the person I was before my journey began, and it is only now, in my mid-thirties, that I have finally come to understand and love who I am. I love myself for every trait I encompass—positive, annoying, odd, silly, weird, unique—all the characteristics that make me who I am. Taking the time to discover my inner being has been the best thing I have ever done next to becoming a mother.

METAMORPHOSIS

If I could stress one thing more than anything else on your own spiritual journey, it would be to never feel selfish for taking the time to learn to love who you are. Some people who are closest to you may not understand your journey, and that's okay. They may tell you you've changed, and they don't recognize you, or that you live in a different reality, and that's okay too. Don't force them to understand how you got to the point of self-discovery and how you found your inner being. You'll know when it's the right time to share what you have learned and how you got there.

Not everyone is on the same plane vibrationally, but I promise that the more you raise your own level, the more it will help others raise theirs. When others see a change for the good, it often inspires them as well. Just as Napoleon Hill explained in defining his principles, enthusiasm is contagious, so always make sure what you're spreading is positive. If people are ready to share in the experience, they will accept it with open arms.

In understanding universal laws, self-healing, and manifestation, everyone must find their own time to rediscover the meaning of who they are and who they are meant to be. You cannot force the process of finding another's definite major purpose. You cannot drag someone along the path of least resistance with you if they are still mired in the past.

The transition can only happen for those who are ready to leave behind old beliefs, limitations, negative thought patterns, low self-confidence, and doubt. Doubt is the enemy of all things dreamt, the turbulent winds tearing down the sails. When someone is willing to change, they will know it within, setting fire to the desires buried deep beneath the feelings of "I can't" or "it will never happen."

In everything I learned, it was first through awareness that I understood how powerful I was. That through use of the "three tiers to vibrational alignment", as I call it, anything and everything can change for the better. There is no "I can't" or "it will never happen" in my book of dreams and desires.

The three tiers to vibrational alignment consist of three levels one must achieve to reach a place that brings forth the accomplishment of your dreams. The first tier, *awareness,* is the first step in understanding the process of the Law of Attraction and recognizing that you have unknowingly manifested wherever you are now.

Awareness helps to bring realization that you are what you think and that the way you've been thinking, acting, feeling, and living has created your current reality. Like attracts like, regardless of the thought, which makes awareness of thought the most important part of the first tier.

The second tier is *reflected healing.* Working through repressed issues, you're able to see the foundation of what is blocking you from the greatness that lives within you, the same greatness that lives in all of us. Every single one of us has a definite major purpose inside, regardless of our race, sex, religion, or social status.

We are all destined to add to the beauty of the world we live in. However, we can never open the gift within us if it's blocked by past traumas or regrets clinging to the fibers of our being.

Reflecting on our aches and pains, understanding the parts of life we've refused to let go of, and releasing pent-up hurt will cause a pool of peace we can immerse ourselves in. If I hadn't been able to sit back and take the time to really listen to what was bothering me, the actual reasons for my anxieties, I would have never been able to reach the last tier, *absolute alignment.*

The third and final tier, which brings forth the manifestations placed inside the vortex, is the greatest feeling in the world. It feels so good to be in complete sync with my inner being that the clarity and inspiration I receive as a result elate me more each day. Some days, they bring me to joyous tears.

Everything in life feels so much easier. More fluid. Life is flowing so strongly and effortlessly with the current that I'm finally able to enjoy all the sights along the way. Synchronicity is an everyday occurrence. The norm. And when it happens, I smile, knowing that I attracted it.

Colors seem brighter. Scents are more intense. Love feels stronger. And even though it took strength to dig myself out of the rubble, as soon as I forgave myself for all the things I had done, I understood who I was, which allowed me to connect to who I truly am. I understood my reactions, bad habits, and stubborn capabilities. I understood why I had done the things I had in life, even allowing myself to be sucked into the substance abuse that consumed me for so long. Everything made sense, which made *absolute alignment* that much more profound.

It's so easy to get stuck on limitations that sometimes the answers that are trying to find us can't get through. The walls built high by our belief that we cannot change or be who we really want to be hide the idea that prosperity and abundance are there for the taking. Always. Nobody can attest to that more than I.

Trapped by the belief that only bad things happened to me because of my innate faults, I could not detect the seedlings desperate to grow inside of me, showing me that life can be good. Life can be wondrous, exciting, and kind. I needed only to accept that I was only human and that humans can learn and grow from their mistakes, rather than being continually punished for them.

Following the three tiers to vibrational alignment helped me to come to my senses, and for that, I am forever grateful. Now, when little things pop up, and they will, it's just a part of life. I step back and take time to reflect in order to determine the right resolution. By using everything I've learned from all the amazing mentors that have helped to guide me along the way, I bounce back quicker and stronger.

I thank the unproductive thought, always, just as Gabrielle suggested in *Super Attractor*, and then dissect it in a way that leads me to a better understanding of what I want to attract instead. I don't seek to place blame anywhere other than myself, because, after all is said and done, I am responsible for my own reactions.

I don't waste time and energy on small matters of unimportance, but if something is really blocking me, I take time to rest and refocus in a way that involves self-care. I read, sleep late if I can, take Epsom salt baths, and watch affirming videos.

I also listen to music to switch my mood, watch stand-up comedy, treat myself to a spa day at home, and *always* indulge in "the works" shower. Created by a friend and former coworker, the works consists of everything under the sun: shampoo, conditioner, scrub, shave, and whatever else you use to pamper yourself in the stall of rejuvenation. I do some of my best thinking in the shower, and most times, I find a directional solution to help bring me closer back to realignment.

If I'm out in public where a peaceful space and time alone are not available, I use "secret shifters," an idea pulled from one of my favorite books, *The Secret*. I think of wonderful memories or things I love, like the beach, to modify my solemn or anxious feeling immediately. Sometimes, it only takes but a minute to change the direction of an unwanted feeling if you focus on one of your secret shifters. Keep thinking of things that excite you or make you happy until you feel a shift in your vibration.

Regardless of where you are, do whatever it takes to get yourself back on track. Work out, cook, treat yourself to lunch. Do anything that offers feelings of peace, love, and restoration. There will be times when you're set back, and the best thing about being set back is that you can always feel the difference and when it's time to make a shift.

You can always tell when you're in sync with your inner being and when you're not. Once you become aware of who you really are, you'll immediately know what end of the spectrum you're sitting on at any point in your day.

The best thing to do when faced with unbalanced waves of emotion is to regain your composure. Relax and practice everything you've learned. It will help recenter you and bring you to a place where your thoughts are quiet enough that you can hear which way you should go.

Taking the time to calm your mind may feel like you're not doing anything to promote closure between yourself and whatever is in your vortex. It may feel as though you're wasting time that could be put toward serving your definite major purpose, but I promise, even though it feels like you're not doing anything, you are. You are clearing out the clutter in your mind so you can get back to the point of clarity received through alignment with your inner being. Clearing things out so you can hear and feel Source energy guiding you to make clearer decisions will benefit both you and the interactions you have with others.

Don't worry about how much of your vibration was lost. You didn't lose all of it. It's still there waiting for you. If you rush to get back to where you were, you'll put more obstacles in your path. As Abraham-Hicks says, "You are where you are." Know that each day is new. Fresh. A chance to switch momentum moving forward in the positive.

Do start your morning with positive thinking. Pray, write, listen to calming music. Watch a funny video or listen to your favorite inspirational speaker sharing new insights to help you grow. If it helps you get going, make a focus wheel with what you want to do. Meditating is another great way to jumpstart your day.

Abraham-Hicks shares that it's important to meditate when your mind is clear and not cluttered. When we focus on not thinking about the things we're trying to forget, we often accelerate those thoughts. Focus on simple things when meditating, like your breath or the humming of the fridge. Abraham-Hicks explains it's the little things that require the least amount of thought that help take us to a quiet space where we can be open to receiving clarity.

The times when I've been calm enough during meditation to really stop and quiet my mind, feelings of joy have overwhelmed me. In those moments, I see my biggest desires and feel as though I am actually living them in the present. In those times of absolute clarity and awareness, I know I am connecting with Source and in perfect alignment with my inner being.

You will find what works best for you and what doesn't with getting back into alignment. If you're focusing on what threw you off from the day before, you're setting yourself up for a place I promise you don't want to go to. Like a small snowball at the top of a snowy hill, the more you keep nudging it, the better the chances that it will roll down without your full consent, gathering more snow along the way. Before you know it, the little ball is a giant mass you can't even see over.

Always give yourself time to breathe. Time to think. Don't beat yourself up about feeling out of alignment, either. The step I loved most out of Abraham-Hicks's five-step process was step five. I used to cry whenever I was set back to step one. In fact, I did just the other day, even though I knew there was no reason to work myself up over the setback.

Even with all the work I've put in, I still have times when I cry and release what I don't need. Then I pull myself together and tell myself that it's okay. I reassure my mind that I'm safe and I haven't undone all my hard work. I've only stumbled a bit, and once the sting wears off, the discomfort will subside, and I will be just fine.

Some days just feel crappy, and that's to be expected. With everything going on in the world today, setbacks seem to occur more frequently. But it's up to us to use those setbacks in ways that serve us. Relationships fall apart, jobs are lost, health issues pop up, traumatic triggers get the best of you some days, financial resources can dwindle, and it feels like everything is working against you. Greatness can be born during those times. Feel what needs to be felt, hear what's needed to be heard, and release that shit. Don't dwell.

It's important to be the coach you need when you're trailing behind by a few points or a lot of points. Self-encouragement is more helpful than you think. It's the pat on the back when you need reassurance. Ask for a sign from your guides or the Universe. That helps too. I always ask in times where I feel alone, afraid, or frustrated.

It's important that when you ask for help, you listen to what is being offered. You want to show your guides that you're listening when they speak. Anytime I ask for help, like if I feel afraid, I'll then glance at the stove and see one of my numbers or see something from my list of significant signs and know that my spirit guides are helping to redirect me.

Often, it's instant and I know that in that moment, even though I may be feeling down, that I am still open to the connection of receiving their help, and I take it. Always.

However, if you find yourself mired in quicksand, slowly sinking whenever you try to move, never make any big decisions or start a new project. You'll only complicate matters and feel frustrated things are not flowing as easily as they usually do.

When you *are* in a place of receiving (alignment), it is crucial to trust in the power that lives inside of you. When you feel a new idea or a great thought come to mind, that is Source recognizing your alignment and sending you new things to be inspired about. Allowing and acknowledging the inspiration only brings more of it.

Stop what you're doing and write down the thoughts and ideas that come to you. In that moment when you receive, never take it for granted and never push it aside. I love when I write down new inspirations or desires and then turn to look at the time and see one of my angel numbers from my spirit guides. It's like receiving a high five from your teammate after scoring the winning goal.

Once you gain trust within yourself and build a relationship of well-being and productive thoughts, it's important to never doubt when you hear your inner voice calling you. If your ego pops up, trying to tell you that what you're thinking is outlandish or impossible, push back. Tell your ego that you're not interested anymore.

It may feel like you're dealing with an old lover who keeps phoning and begging you to take them back when it comes to the tug-of-war game with your ego. That's just your old habits calling, seeking to get your attention. But don't pick up! Let the machine get it. Keep trying and don't give up. There is always a way to leave your ego in the dust when it's unwelcomed.

As my dear friend explains, you can tell the difference between your ego and your inner self. Our egos have a way of finding us during our setbacks, even when we gain good momentum, and trying to prevent us from moving forward in productivity and wellness.

As soon as I see my ego peeking through my windows from outside, instead of hiding behind the curtain, I twist open the blinds and firmly tell it that there's no vacancy for it today. That it will have to go back where it came from because the house of my mind only takes guests that pay with realism and accuracy. That outdated phobias and anxieties have no business here and that waiting for space to become available will only result in utter disappointment.

Sometimes, I need help with turning away my ego at the front door, but when I do, I embrace the guidance of others with open arms. I never give in to a belief that I am weak and have failed. Instead, I take it as an opportunity to discover something new that I could not sense on my own.

I am grateful for all the help I've received from family and friends and my partner over the years. I know that with the help of my dear friend, guiding me on a spiritual level, I will continue to get to a place of enlightenment and higher peace.

Allowing yourself to connect to others who are also working to raise their vibrational level may be more beneficial than trying to do everything on your own. However, there's a difference between guidance that comes from a place of well-being and guidance that comes from judgment. It is my understanding from listening to Napoleon Hill teach his principles, that all judgment is a negative thought about another person's opinions, thoughts, beliefs, or desires, and, once shared with another, it can create what I call the "double dose effect."

Not only is the judgmental thought internalized by the person who created it, springing a leak on their own vibration, but it also alters the perceptional vibration of the person being judged. That's why awareness of what you are offering for guidance is so important. Phrases like "I would never," "why would you ever," and "that's stupid" only hurt the person you're trying to "help."

Let people be who they are. The goal is not to make another feel inferior. Remember that if someone asks for your help, give judgment-free guidance. That way, you can be a light trying to brighten their life.

Judgment weakens the worldly vibration of togetherness that we have worked so hard to get over the years. If we could learn to value all that we separately bring to the universal table that we all dine at, perhaps we would see differences subside in a way that casts out all feelings of judgment. When we learn to appreciate those around us, even if they are "different," nobody is silenced or judged. Everyone wants and deserves to be heard. Everyone.

So, armed with the concept that potlucks bring more variety into our family feasts, I consciously accept all the characteristics of the people I love, favorable and unfavorable alike. But don't confuse "unfavorable" with "tolerable." Some people just need to be released.

I think it's easy in relationships to get frustrated with one another when you are on different vibrations. Instead, know that the catch-up game is a patient process, and if you love someone enough to share your life with them and you can see they're slowly making gains, you will continue your work, knowing that helping yourself helps them. But if the person you love isn't progressing, and you sense a shift in yourself that doesn't feel good, reevaluate.

Sometimes the best thing you can do for everyone involved is release the relationship altogether.

Keep in mind that what is done to one is done to another. Looking at relationship quarrels from that perspective really changes what disagreements are worth pursuing and what is worth letting go. That goes for everyone in your life: spouse, family, friends, coworkers, and even your children.

Since starting this journey, I've grown so much closer to my son. As I continue to teach him the ways of the Universe and how deliberate thinking helps us in our creation, this has done wonders for him. In fact, this Mother's Day, in the homemade card he makes every year, he thanked me for teaching him about the laws of the Universe.

De'Andre is a child who needs constant redirection and attention, and I've learned to understand his traits and what I need to give and teach him as a mother. My goal is to help him learn independence and confidence; to understand that he can do and be anything he wants in life with the right concepts to guide him.

So I approach him in ways that I know he'll understand, and I don't overreact to his behavior. Some days are easier than others, but as a mother who used to lose her temper during extreme moments in parenting, I have since let go of my bad behavior, wanting to teach my son and myself more calming ways to deal with our frustrations.

Kids learn their behaviors through observation. Travis Hirschi, a well-known criminal theorist who studied the connection between social bonding and criminalization, concluded that our children are a duplication of who we are because they mimic what they see. Whether or not we want to admit it, they are the best and worst parts of us.

The beliefs that we carry and pass down to them will either help or hurt them. Bonding with our children in a way that doesn't project our fears, worries, or prejudices onto them is crucial for the peaceful evolution of our future world. If you want to change and shift something within your child, you first need to establish a shift in yourself.

As soon as I reined in my own neediness, anger, and expectation that others should make me happy, I noticed slight changes take place in my son. He slowed down more to hear what I was saying and listened better to the new ways of thinking I was teaching him. Before I knew it, he was sharing his own stories of the Law of Attraction and what he had manifested.

When De'Andre and I go for walks now, we talk about all the wonderful things we will have in our new home: a mansion by the water, a pool, a garden, a "man cave." He even picks out the colors that we'll paint on his bedroom walls and designs a whole sound system setup with speakers and percussion so he can make music in his room.

Creating with others is fun once you realize that you're not just fantasizing but actually attracting the desires that captivate you. I enjoy collecting pictures of my dream home online. I created a digital vision board on my phone with a photo album dedicated to how my home will look and the things I want to furnish it with. I go online to Zillow and take screenshots of fabulous mansions off the coast of Florida filled with scenic coastal views of tropical turquoise waters.

There is something about the ocean that makes me feel peaceful. Whenever my toes touch the wet sand and the water trickles in around them, I feel I'm where I belong. Every time I see the different shades of blue and green mixing into an expanding vastness that looks never-ending, I get so warm inside. It presents a sea of possibilities waiting for me to grab hold. Each time I watch a new wave rolling in, new opportunities are being brought forth to inspire me.

Creating is a joyful activity, but there may be times when you wonder if those around you, who are not on the same vibrational level, can burst a hole in your vortex. Abraham-Hicks said, "If man understood that 'what I create has nothing to do with what anybody else is creating,' then he wouldn't be so afraid of what others are doing," which is the perfect thought pattern to fall back on.

So don't worry about what others are creating or not creating. If we become preoccupied with the vibrations that others are on, it prevents us from raising our own. A true empath, I can attest to how unproductive it is when we get tangled up in what others are feeling. Empathy is good if used in a way to understand that someone needs a little extra space, that they're going through a tough time, or that something you've done or said has affected them.

If, like me, you are someone who is constantly aware of what others are emotionally going through, please remember that it's not your job to heal someone else's pain. Your job is only to love and support those who need it, when they need it, the best you can without disrupting your own path to alignment.

It is my belief that we are the creators of our own reality and that, through the Law of Attraction, we bring what we are thinking into our lives. That we can be "magnets for Divine Prosperity," as Louise Hay said, and all things abundant if we understand the infinite power of the Universe and the power that's inside us.

It is also my belief that there is a whole other spirit world that exists among the living of those who have crossed over. That archangels and spirit guides watch over us, supporting every step we take in life. And that the spiritual help that is offered to all can only be used by those who resonate on the vibrational level that accepts that help and who also *believe*.

If I could make suggestions to anyone who is ready to learn about the majestic force of attraction, to learn about the power within to heal wounds that create blockages, to discover their inner being and receive the most incredible clarity, I would suggest reading the following books, watching the following videos, and subscribing to the following YouTube channels in this specific order:

1. Rhonda Byrne: *The Secret*
2. Louise Hay: *You Can Heal Your Life*
3. Napoleon Hill: *Master Key*
4. Gabrielle Bernstein: *Super Attractor*
5. Bob Proctor: YouTube channel (Now Proctor Gallagher Institute)
6. Abraham-Hicks: YouTube channel

I would also suggest making a list of affirmations[16] that will help serve you personally. Tailoring affirmations to sing or say to yourself in times of fear is more effective than reacting on the spot.

Simply take the fear that you hold and reword it in its opposite form. For instance, if there is a constant thought of getting sick, the affirming thought could be, "I am full of health. Health flourishes inside of me daily."

Every negative or unproductive thought has a positive affirmation. *You Can Heal Your Life* offers wonderful lists of affirming thoughts. Learning from the best of hers, I've since created a ton for myself. Some I only needed for a short time, and others for a little longer. Either way, have fun with it.

Dance around the house as you sing your new, uplifting thoughts. Sing at the top of your lungs, doing dance moves you wouldn't want your best friends to see you do! Just go with it and create whatever feels good to you as you release what no longer serves you.

There's nothing I love more than when I'm rapping my affirmation out loud to a beat in my head, jumping up and down, twerking, or even doing the running man and then looking over to see 11:11 or any of my other numbers popping up on the TV or digital clock.

However you choose to affirm or heal, I bet that in a year's time, if the work has been internalized and correctly done, you will see a significant difference in your life. People will enter your life that you never expected. You will see new opportunities present themselves in ways that not only feel amazing but deserved. You will see new ideas and inspirations sprout up daily, helping you to discover new purposes in life to help others and further launch your own success.

You will see that everything you once feared burns away like a mound of dry hay. Once you reach the point where your fears are powerless over you and what you choose to think of instead, you will see life in a way that allows you to live in abundance: health, love, success, wealth, and more.

When I used to feel bad, I felt empty. I was hungry for something more. Once I healed and increased my spirituality in ways I never expected, I felt full . . . always! Now, my eyes are bigger than my stomach! I crave all sorts of things in life and that's what life is about . . . living. It's about following your dreams and desiring many things that move and inspire you.

Throughout this journey, I have learned about the power that lives in all of us. The power that gives us the ability to live and create, to be anything we want. It doesn't matter where you've been, where you are, or where you've always wanted to be. All of what you want and then some can be yours for the taking, *if* you believe it exists.

So, in conclusion, I share with you the following personal thoughts.

Always stay positive and dream big. It's never too late to accomplish the things you desire. I'm thirty-five, just graduated from college, and am about to embark on the career of my dreams. Writing moves me. It never feels like work, and that's what you want. Love what you wake up and get paid to do every morning. If you don't, then go back to the drawing board and figure out what other job will make you feel happy and fulfilled.

The jobs that we despise are the stepping stones to what we desire. For years, I dreaded going to work and felt miserable five days a week, but I'm so thankful for that experience because it propelled me to make a drastic change and to reexamine what I was doing with my life. It brought me to the realization that I wanted to finish college and write books.

Don't be afraid of change and remember that stepping outside your comfort zone will be well worth it if you are dedicated to go the extra mile and refuse to stop until you've reached your goal. Shoot down barriers that try to stop you. Push through adversity! The only thing that can stop you from achieving your goals and following your passions is you.

Never let anything or anyone knock you down from where you stand for the things you've done or haven't done in life. Mistakes can be forgiven. I know in my heart that Damin forgives me for not being the person I wanted to be when he knew me. I hope that one day those I have hurt or led down a path of judgmental opinions can look past the person I was then and know that I wasn't strong enough to be who I am today.

We all wish we could undo the negative things we've done in life and make everything right, but the reality is we can never go back and relive life. We can only move forward, which means letting go of the unproductive person you once were and starting a new birthing process of who and what you know you have the potential to be.

Live your life *excitedly*. Do the things that please you and refrain from doing the things that don't. Use the material items you bought to enjoy. I used to be a saver. I saved every piece of new clothing, makeup, even cool dinner plates for "special occasions." The reality is that every day is a special occasion no matter what's going on! Don't wait to use the things you love. You *are* a special occasion.

If you have a pile of unused items, give them away. Giving feels great, especially to someone who you know will cherish things just as much as you did when you were first moved to buy them.

Give thanks for all you have. Every day I say thank you for everything I have in life. Even if it's a text from a friend I haven't heard from for a while, or watching the trees blow in the wind. I thank the eyes I have to see and the legs I have to walk. I also give thanks for the food as I'm cooking it, no matter how long the prep time takes for my family's favorite meal. Everything deserves thanks in life, and that's something we all forget from time to time.

That said, being thankful is never about comparing yourself to others and what they have gained from their "vortex." It's about recognizing all that *you* have manifested in yours.

Don't rush things! Rushing never gets you what you want when you want it. Trust in the timing of your manifestations. Never launch something until it's ready: a proposal, a product, an invention, a book. I can reflectively look back and see how I hurried the first two manuscripts I wrote. Rushing is the pathway to all things sloppy. It may take a little longer to get things done right, but when all is said and done, the extra hard work will pay off.

"Going the extra mile," as Napoleon Hill reminds us, is an old school saying that honestly bears the biggest, boldest fruit from the labor tree. Making sure things are perfect is not just about pride. It's about selling your ideas in a way that no one can turn them down.

A few days after I finished this manuscript, *Metamorphosis*, I couldn't wait to submit it, but C.J. reminded me not to rush the process. So I took time to perfect it. I polished it like an apple given to a teacher on the first day of school. I bought a book on finding agents and how to write a slam dunk proposal. I sent the manuscript through three copy edits, one with the help of my mother and the other with a local professional whom I attracted in the most amazing way! I even took a writer's workshop put on by Hay House.

Remember that spiritual help is all around us at all times. Call out to your guides and ask for guidance! Every morning when I pray and give thanks for the day I'm about to begin, I always invite my guides and guardians in. I ask for their help in the things I want to do that day and know they will be there to support me, showing me signs along the way.

The cool thing about prayer is that you can do it anywhere, anytime. Pray to *your* Source for anything and everything. Build that connection and trust so when you are out of alignment, you feel comfortable enough to reach out to the magnificent energy that Source provides and ask for help.

I like to think of it as a group effort in which they help. Daily. Once you gain that perspective, prayer is not a chore that has to be done, but something you'll want to do because it feels good.

For the longest time, having gone to Catholic school, I felt that prayer was more of an obligation than a spiritual connection. I'm so glad that I have found a new light in praying. I enjoy doing it and have developed a prayer routine[17] that I say every morning. Whether I'm still in bed, cooking breakfast, or in the shower, I always start my morning off with prayer when I have a couple of moments to myself and give thanks for the guiding signs I know I'll receive throughout the day.

In the beginning, when I asked for signs, I felt a little like a child constantly nagging their parent for the same thing every day. It's important to know that your guides will always give support, and it's never an issue to ask for too much. They will deliver at times that surprise you and other times when you sit back and say, "I knew you were going to do that for me."

Like the time when I received the thank you card with the beautiful purple flowers and butterflies on it. Before I even pulled out the card, I knew that there would be purple flowers, but my guides one-upped my intuition and added purple butterflies. I laughed and thanked them for the kind gesture, knowing that they were proud of me for helping to bring comfort to another by sharing the gift of Louise's book, *You Can Heal Your Life*.

Pay attention to the signs. Keep track and look up their meaning as they come along. They will allow a unique form of confidence to flow through you. Resonating consistently on a frequency that allows me to receive, I can say that since I've come to a place of stronger alignment, the number signs I receive have nearly tripled. Sometimes, I get four different number signs in less than a minute's time.

Finally, always remember that thoughts of positivity attract new clarity, new inspiration, new growth, new circumstances, new achievement, and new opportunities. Each day has a new sun that illuminates new experiences. Embrace every morning with excitement, knowing that wherever you are, you have the chance to increase your vibration even more with the thoughts and emotions you choose to focus on.

As I sit here writing the closing paragraphs of this book, I feel giddy thinking of all the things I can do next. Maybe I'll write a book about numerology and signs. I do know that I'll write a follow-up to *Metamorphosis*. The years' time it took from when I finished the book with my first editor and when it was published, well, that's a whole other story that must be told! I love knowing that anything I want to experience in life is obtainable. And I love knowing that the possibilities of what *I* can create in *my* life are endless.

Always remember that you determine the colors that will go on your canvas. You have control over how bright or dull your paint strokes are. Know that each one of us, including you, has a special purpose to better serve others and the wider world. Never, ever doubt that. So, together, let us change ourselves and the world one positive thought at a time.

Well wishes,
Ashley

End Notes

[1] *"Habit of going the extra mile"* Going the extra mile would separate one's abilities from another's and would heavily dictate the outcome of the intended achievement. Creating a formula called "QQMA," the *quality* and *quantity* of the service plus the *mental attitude* of achieving it would bring increased returns. In addition, it would also gather attention from those who could provide the right opportunities, at the right time.

[2] *"Applied faith"* Mentally shaping one's attitude in a way that washed away all fear and doubt so focus could be drawn to the desired accomplishment. Applying faith was the ticket to overcoming any failure that tried to tackle one while in motion. It helped to maintain control of the mind through positive thoughts.

[3] *"Pleasing personality"* A pleasing personality would set one apart from others by showing off their personal characteristics. When placed in the position to draw others near for assistance, personality traits would either promote people to help, or prompt them to flee. Facial expressions and tone of voice were clear indicators if one had a pleasing personality or a less pleasant one.

[4] *"Self-discipline"* Self-discipline involved remembering that what was pushed onto others in anger ultimately would be pushed back. Controlling emotions in uncomfortable situations, self-discipline acted as a shield against losing power to matters of unimportance.

5. *"Positive mental attitude"* Starting each day with laughter and setting the brain chemistry to an exceptional level would help put one in a position for positivity. Following morning laughter with praise and thankfulness for the day's intended attractions would also raise one to a place of higher vibration and create a positive mental attitude.
6. *"Enthusiasm"* Enthusiasm not only helped on an individual level but was an aid for others as well. Contagious, both good and bad, enthusiasm would spread like dandelion seeds blown by the wind, transmitting one's vibration out into the world.
7. *"Personal initiative"* The individual push to finish what was started, personal initiative placed responsibility on one to carry out their *own* definite major purpose. Taking action without being told what to do by others and not stopping till the job was done.
8. *"Learning from adversity"* Finding positivity in disappointments and failures and translating them into blessings. Productiveness in adversity would set one up for inspiration that might not be found otherwise, providing the opportunity for another stone to step on.
9. *"Creative vision"* Responsible for generating plans for the desired outcome through imagination, there were two types to be considered. *Synthetic* imagination was taking old ideas and creating newer and more successful ones. *Created* imagination, stored in the subconscious, was accessed through the sixth sense. Both were important, as creativity stood as the foundation to success.
10. *"Accurate thinking"* The ability to differentiate between matters of importance and unimportance. Not wasting time on insignificant issues that repelled positivity. Focusing on factual information versus assumption by hypotheses. Accurate thinking led one closer to the definite major purpose by giving attention where it belonged.

[11] *"Cosmic habit force"* A natural law sustaining the balance of the Universe, cosmic habit force set attainment in motion through one's habitual patterns. Definitive action stemmed from one's patterns of instinct, attracting contents from either envelope presented at birth. Mastering the force would allow one to determine the type of action produced through proper mind control in order to seek desirable attainment.

[12] Tropical Turmeric Smoothie: Two chunks of frozen cherries, two slices of frozen banana, two chunks of frozen pineapple, one scoop organic vanilla protein powder, 1 tbsp organic chia seeds, 1 tbsp organic ground flax seed, 6 drops of liquid organic sweetener, 1 scoop Innate Turmeric Response Powder. Blend until well mixed, serve in a frosted glass, and enjoy!

[13] Magnificent Hot Matcha Latte: Fill favorite mug with 8 oz of preferred milk; I use almond milk. Dump into pot and bring to boil on stove. Add capful of vanilla flavoring. Add preferred amount of liquid sweetener; I use about 8 drops. Once milk has boiled, add 1-2 tsp of matcha powder; I use Superfood by MRM, matcha green tea powder. Whisk well until powder is dissolved. Allow to simmer for 1-2 minutes. Remove from heat, add a dash of sea salt and one splash of organic, heavy creamer. Let cool for a few minutes before stirring and enjoy!

[14] Abraham-Hicks's twelve beliefs:

1. "You are a physical extension of that which is nonphysical."
2. "You are here in this body because you choose to be here."
3. "The basis of your life is freedom; the purpose of your life is joy."
4. "You are a creator; you create with your every thought."
5. "Anything that you can imagine is yours to be or do or

have."
6. "As you are choosing your thoughts, your emotions are guiding you."
7. "The Universe adores you for it knows your broadest intentions."
8. "Relax into your natural well-being. All is well. (Really it is!)"
9. "You are a creator of thought ways on your unique path of joy."
10. "Actions to be taken and possessions to be exchanged are byproducts of your focus on joy."
11. "You may appropriately depart your body without illness or pain."
12. "You cannot die; you are everlasting life."

[15] "Rocket of Desire" Strong, fast, temporary desire that has been orchestrated through contrasted experiences and launched into one's vortex. Since the desire is new, the frequency has not yet been mastered so it is not in reach vibrationally. Practicing what has been learned through deliberate thinking will help one move a little closer each day toward the frequency of the new desire launched, eventually lining one up when the vibration is has been equally matched.

[16] List of affirmations: Here are some personally tailored affirmations. Some are favorites that I have discovered from my mentors.

1. "I am grateful for my home and all the joy it provides." (If unhappy with your current living situation.)
2. "Good things are on the way." (Abraham-Hicks)
3. "Things are always getting better." (Abraham-Hicks)
4. "I am a magnet for golden opportunities." (Louise Hay)
5. "My body is healthy; my body is safe." (For those who fear

illness or disease.)
6. "I heal my body more each day. I am a health regenerator!" (Again, for health.)
7. "I have a constant flow of financial funds. My funds are unlimited." (When worried about finances.)
8. "There is safety all around me. Every place I go, and travel to." (Helps with driving and for those who struggle with populated, public places.)
9. "My family and I are safe and healthy. We are protected." (Good for those recovering from traumatic events.)
10. "Things *always* work out for my family and me. We attract all things good." (Works wonders when experiencing family difficulty.)
11. "I bless _____ with flourishing love." (Someone I want to pray for and send positivity their way. Great affirmation when dealing with disagreement with others.)
12. "I am safe. I am secure. I am health." (My go-to, daily "I am" mantra. I have a special song and dance for this one!)

[17] Morning Prayer: "Dear God, I thank you for this day you have given me. I am thankful for _____. I ask you to continue to help heal me and ask that you dissolve anything that doesn't serve my body and mind. I ask that you flourish all the health continuing to grow inside of me. I call upon my spirit guides and guardians and grant them permission to better guide and protect me. I ask for signs throughout the day and thank everyone for their help and support. Help me to be stronger than I was yesterday. Amen."

Bibliography

BEAUTYCOUNTER

BEAUTYCOUNTER. (2020). *Our Story*. Retrieved June 27, 2020, from https://www.beautycounter.com/our-mission

Gabrielle Bernstein

Bernstein, Gabrielle. (2019). *Super Attractor*. Pgs. Intro, 8-9, 13, 102-121, Hay House, Inc.

YouTube. (2019). *Gabrielle Bernstein on Healing Trauma and Spiritual Freedom with Lewis Howes*. Retrieved June 2, 2020, from https://www.youtube.com/watch?v=yrjztUx2hxM&t=2167s

YouTube. (2019). *The Universe Has Your Back*. Retrieved June 2, 2020, from https://www.youtube.com/watch?v=_vSwDvej25M&t=54s

Rhonda Byrne

The Secret. (2020). *Rhonda Byrne's Biography*. Retrieved May 9, 2020, from https://www.thesecret.tv/about/rhonda-byrnes-biography/

The Secret. (2020). *History of The Secret*. Retrieved May 9, 2020, from https://www.thesecret.tv/about/history-of-the-secret/

Byrnes, Rhonda. (2006). *The Secret, 10th Universe Edition.* Creste LLC. Pgs. 1-22, 29, 31-32, 37, 45-57, 60-67, 72, 78-80, 95-97, 102-107, 128, 136-137, 143, 187, 190, 194-195.

Byrnes, Rhonda. (2006). *The Secret, 10th Universe Edition.* Creste LLC. Pgs. 37.

Jack Canfield

Chicken Soup for the Soul. (2020). *Facts and figures.* Retrieved May 21, 2020, from https://www.chickensoup.com/about/facts-and-figures

YouTube. (2018). *How to Reject Rejection.* Jack Canfield. Retrieved May 26, 2020, from https://www.youtube.com/watch?v=IZkR3ym6wVU&t=6s

YouTube. (2019). *THE META SECRET (LAW OF ATTRACTION) FULL MOIVE.* Thinker: The Creator. Retrieved May 26, 2020, from https://www.youtube.com/watch?v=mjmK8aJu5Qg&t=349s

YouTube. (n.d.). *THE META SECRET- (FULL MOVIE) LAW OF ATTRACTION.* Power of the mind. Retrieved May 30, 2022, from https://www.youtube.com/watch?v=i7GmSg8vmcg&t=1298s

Andrew Carnegie

History. (2019). *Andrew Carnegie.* Retrieved May 26, 2020, from https://www.history.com/topics/19th-century/andrew-carnegie

Louise Hay

Louise Hay. (n.d.). *About*. Retrieved June 3, 2020, from https://www.louisehay.com/

Louise Hay. (1999). *You Can Heal Your Life*. Pgs. 16, 18-19, 21-22, 111, 136, 141, 143, 231-236. Hay House Inc.

Napoleon Hill Master Key, Unlocking the Secret to Success, Wealth & Happiness

Amazon. (1954). *Napoleon Hill's Master Key Unlocking the Secret to Success, Wealth & Happiness*. Retrieved May 9, 2020, from https://www.amazon.com/Napoleon-Hills-Master-Key/dp/B01J2UYIBK?ref_=nav_ya_signin&

Famous Authors. (2020). Napoleon Hill. Retrieved May 26, 2020, from https://www.famousauthors.org/napoleon-hill

Google Books. (2016). Napoleon Hill's Gold Standard: An Official Publication of The Napoleon Hill Foundation. Retrieved June 3, 2020, from https://books.google.com/books?id=fjesDAAAQBAJ&pg=PT153&lpg=PT153&dq=was+napoleon+hill+born+into+poverty&source=bl&ots=rAVSLeUVkk&sig=ACfU3U31Pkr_v6rrGsmkT0FS1ND0hY3Z5w&hl=en&sa=X&ved=2ahUKEwi2juH7gubpAhUsTd8KHXSIC_8Q6AEwEXoECBMQAQ#v=onepage&q=was%20napoleon%20hill%20born%20into%20poverty&f=false

Napoleon Hill Foundation. (2020). Think and Grow Rich. Retrieved May 30, 2020, from https://www.naphill.org/shop/books/think-and-grow-rich/

Lisa Nichols

Motivating the Masses. (2020). About Lisa Nichols. Retrieved May 18, 2020, from https://www.motivatingthemasses.com/about/

Motivating the Masses. (2022). About Lisa Nichols. Retrieved August 26, 2022, from https://motivatingthemasses.com/about/lisa-nichols/

Thought Definition

Merriam Webster. (2020). Thought. Retrieved May 18, 2020, from https://www.merriam-webster.com/dictionary/thought

Bob Proctor

YouTube. (2019). *You Squared: Create Your Own Quantum Leap.* Proctor Gallagher Institute. Retrieved June 3, 2020, from https://www.youtube.com/watch?v=XRr-t961_Qw

Gina Self

Gina Self Psychic Medium. (n.d.). *About me*. Retrieved June 7, 2020, from https://www.ginaself.com/about-me.html

W. Clement Stone

Amazon. (2020). W. Clement Stone. Retrieved May 9, 2020, from https://www.amazon.com/W.-Clement-Stone/e/B000APTR4A%3Fref=dbs_a_mng_rwt_scns_share

Abraham-Hicks

Abraham-Hicks Publication. (2020). *About Abraham*. Retrieved June 20, 2020, from https://www.abraham-hicks.com/about/

Amazon. (2020). Ask and It Is Given: Learning to Manifest Your Desires. Retrieved June 20, 2020, from https://www.amazon.com/Ask-Given-Learning-Manifest-Desires/dp/1401904599

YouTube. (2020). *Abraham-Hicks 2020-Expect Only Good Things For Yourself, And You Will Be Shocked By The Response*. Retrieved June 29, 2020, from https://www.youtube.com/watch?v=2eZMjpFevMY

YouTube. (2013). *Abraham Hicks- For Beginners . . . What is The Vortex? Law of Attraction*. Retrieved June 26, 2020, from https://www.youtube.com/watch?v=MMwl_FNYZFc

YouTube. (2020). *Abraham Hicks- MOST EMPOWERING MESSAGE*. Joyous Journey. Retrieved July 5, 2020, from https://www.youtube.com/watch?v=9JYp-VVVLGA&t=2070s

YouTube. (2019). *Abraham Hicks-The Five Steps Manifesting Your Desires*. Source Inspires. Retrieved June 20, 2020, from https://www.youtube.com/watch?v=WvxYZWC7KHo

YouTube. (2019). *Abraham Hicks What is Your Inner Being*. Inner FreedomSystem. Retrieved June 20, 2020, from https://www.youtube.com/watch?v=dEy0zZcE700

YouTube. (2012). *Abraham Hicks Workshop: You're launching rockets of desire*. The Portal Library. Retrieved July 8, 2020, from https://www.youtube.com/watch?v=PE89z-5k4bo&t=461s

Dave's Killer Bread

Dave's Killer Bread. (2018). *Our History*. Retrieved June 23, 2020, from http://www.daveskillerbread.com/our-history#our-history-1

Dave's Killer Bread. (2022). *About us*. Retrieved May 30, 2022, from https://www.daveskillerbread.com/about-us

Perkins, E. (2021). Cafferty & Scheidegger. *Second Chance employment for ex-cons at Dave's Killer Bread*. Retrieved June 3, 2022, from

https://racinelaw.com/second-chance-employment-for-ex-cons-at-daves-killer-bread/

Hirschi

Alston, Reginald J., Harley, D., & Lenhoff, K. (1995). *Hirschi's Social Control Theory: A Sociological Perspective on Drug Abuse Among Persons with Disabilities*. The Journal of Rehabilitation. Retrieved July 2, 2020, from https://people.uvawise.edu/pww8y/Supplement/-TheoristsSup/SocControlTh/HirSocConThHiBEnc.htm

Number Meanings

The Secret Of The Tarot. (2020). *Number meanings*. Retrieved June 26, 2020, from https://thesecretofthetarot.com/

Rainbow Description

Universe of Symbolism. (2020). Double Rainbow Symbolism. Retrieved July 5, 2020, from https://www.universeofsymbolism.com/rainbow-symbolism.html

Snake Description

Harris, Elena. (2020). Snake Spirit Animal. Spirit Animal. Retrieved July 5, 2020, from https://www.spiritanimal.info/snake-spirit-animal/

About the Author

Ashley Noel is an African American mother, writer, and graduate of Purdue University Global with an AA in criminology and criminal justice. In her free time, she enjoys family and friends, cooking, the beach, exercising, and karaoke. Ashley is a music lover and collector of band tees.

An expert at overcoming obstacles, having beaten drug addiction and alcoholism, PTSD, an eating disorder, and more, Ashley exhibits a strong sense of devotion to helping others in similar situations with her raw, honest style of writing. She is dedicated to making a difference in the world by turning her adversities into a tool to motivate and bring awareness to readers about the power of *self-healing, transformation,* and *successful manifestation.*

Note from the Author

Word-of-mouth is crucial for any author to succeed. If you enjoyed *Metamorphosis*, please leave a review online—anywhere you are able. Even if it's just a sentence or two. It would make all the difference and would be very much appreciated.

Thanks!
Ashley Noel

We hope you enjoyed reading this title from:

www.blackrosewriting.com

Subscribe to our mailing list – *The Rosevine* – and receive **FREE** books, daily deals, and stay current with news about upcoming releases and our hottest authors.
Scan the QR code below to sign up.

Already a subscriber? Please accept a sincere thank you for being a fan of Black Rose Writing authors.

View other Black Rose Writing titles at www.blackrosewriting.com/books and use promo code **PRINT** to receive a **20% discount** when purchasing.